History of China

Spring Books
London - New York - Sydney - Toronto

Concise History of Great Nations
General Editor: Otto Zierer

Otto Zierer China

Contents

1 From Peking Man to Confucius 7
2 Unity and Decay: from the Tsin Dynasty to the Han 22
3 The Threshold of the Middle Ages: the Sui and T'ang Dynasties 33
4 From the Sung Dynasty to the Mongol Invasion 42
5 China becomes Mongol and the Mongols Chinese 51
6 Ming—the Great Brilliance 57
7 The Manchus—Between Past and Present 69
8 The Republic 87
9 Red China 105

Translation by Godfrey Ivins

Dust cover: Emperor K'ang Hsi on a tour of inspection, painting on silk, Manchu period.
Title pages: Demonstration in Red Square (An-men-Tien) in Peking.

Credits:
B. N. Estampes: 8, 9, 10, 11a, b, c, 12, 13, 15, 16, 17, 18, 19, 20a, b, 21, 22/23, 26, 27, 29, 33, 34, 37, 38, 40/41, 43, 44/45, 47, 48, 50 51, 52, 53a, b, c, 55, 58/59, 59, 60a, b, 61, 62, 63, 64/65, 66, 70, 74b, c, 75, 78b, c, 80, 81, 82a, b, c – Giraudon: 86 – Keystone Paris: 4/5, 116, 120 – Musée Guimet: jacket, 24, 32, 35, 49, 69, 71a, b, 72, 73a, b, 74a 76/77, 84/85 – Roger-Viollet: 25, 30, 57, 77, 78a, 79a, b, 82/83, 83, 87, 88/89, 90, 90/91, 91, 93, 94, 95, 96, 97, 98, 99, 108, 109, 112, 113, 114 – V.S.I.S.: 100, 101, 102a, b, 103, 104, 105, 106, 107, 111, 118, 119, 122

Published 1978 by The Hamlyn Publishing Group Limited
London – New York – Sydney – Toronto
Astronaut House, Feltham, Middlesex, England.

ISBN 0 600 32019 7

Printed in Germany by Mohndruck Reinhard Mohn OHG, Gütersloh

1 From Peking Man to Confucius

Old Chinese primers begin with the words: "The sky is blue, the earth is yellow: this is the Middle Kingdom".

Medieval Chinese maps show the "Middle Kingdom" as a rectangle occupying most of the space, while those countries and continents known before the discovery of America form a narrow ornamental fringe around it: Japan and the Sunda Islands, India and Indo-China, Russia and a little of Europe, Persia and part of the Middle East, with an indication of Africa.

For almost 4000 years China has been the most powerful and important civilised land in the Far East, and her influence has extended far beyond her own frontiers.

Bordered by the Yellow Sea in the East, the South China Sea in the South-East, the Himalayas and other major Central Asian mountain ranges, steppes and deserts (such as the Gobi) in the North-West and West, taken with its provinces of Manchuria, Mongolia, Sinkiang, East Turkestan and Tibet, it covers about 3.8 million square miles. The heartland consists of the yellow loess plains and hills of the Yellow River, the Yangtze and the Si-Kiang. This vast land was in ancient times covered with forest right up to the far North, rich in tigers, lions, giant buffalo and elephants. From the very beginning the myth-making imagination of man made it the home of elemental powers such as the yellow dragon, symbolising the mighty, alluvium-rich rivers, the blue dragon, symbolising the sky and typhoons and the red dragon, symbolising storms, fire and catastrophe.

On this broad stage of early history recent investigations by Russian and Chinese archaeologists have discovered in the period more than 100,000 years before the Modern Age a type of primitive man who from the very beginning must have led a settled life, cultivated the soil, raised cattle, kept silkworms, carried out weaving and made pottery.

In 1927 the remains of "Sinanthropus Pekinensis" were found in Chou-k'ou-tien. He was similar to Javan "Picanthropecus Erectus" but clearly distinct from "Giganthopithecus", found in 1935 at Liucheng, and from the African hominids.

In the obscure millennia of early times the aboriginal population of the South and South-West was pushed back and conquered by invaders from North of the Yangtze. The newcomers, also called "Han" Chinese in historical times, had definite strains of Tungus, Mongol, Turki and Tibetan blood in them, were actually Mongols. The southern Chinese, later called "Ming" Chinese, had a strong admixture of Malay and other blood.

About 2000 B.C. a New Stone Age Yang Shao culture appeared in Kansu, Shensi, Shansi and Honan. It produced painted ceramics and spiral patterns which had a certain similarity to the products of prehistoric culture in the Ukraine and the Near East.

About 1800 B.C. there arose the more primitive Lung Shan culture of Shantung and Northern Honan, suggesting connections with Turkestan and Northern Iran. Its typical ceramics are black or grey, sometimes polished and with angular shapes. The position of the finds points to pre-historic migrations of farming populations from West to East.

Everything that Chinese mythology tells us about those early days of civilisation belongs to the realm of legend. The oldest Chinese chronicles tell of three legendary early Emperors: Fu Hsi, who was said to have invented writing, Shen Nung, who is said to have been familiar with the compass, and Huang Ti, who is revered as the "Earth God" and founder of the Chinese empire. Ancient Chinese histories give his dates as 2968 to 2598 B.C.

The Chinese revere the "Five Emperors", or Wu Ti, of primitive times, corresponding to the five elements, metal, water, wood, fire and earth. They were succeeded by the semi-legendary dynasties of the Hsia (2220–1650 B.C.) and the Shang (1650–1122 B.C.).

In the Hsia period agriculture concentrated on rice, millet and wheat, silkworm culture became general, and an early calendar based on units of ten was invented. Side-by-side with this existed a system of counting based on units of twelve, perhaps indicating Babylonian influence.

In the Shang, also called the Yin, period, 30 rulers are listed in the Annals of the Bamboo Books. This was the time of transition between the Stone and Bronze Ages.

A high culture soon developed. Sacrificial vessels, implements of stone, bone, wood and metal were decorated with artistic dragon, bird and snake motifs as well as finely-executed geometrical patterns. The meander pattern points to early Asia Minor influences.

In the Shang period China first clearly showed its national characteristics in the development of its language, script and religion. From the multitude of tribes and peoples of diverse racial origins living in this vast land arose a common culture. The Chinese language is monosyllabic and obtains its rich range of meanings and nuances by means of its tones and compound words. In the course of history a common standard Peking Chinese evolved out of the numerous dialects of the Nanking, Peking, Wu, Fukien or Canton groups. Legend says

that a script was devised in the days of the Emperor Fu Hsi, being derived from the various marks made on the shell of a tortoise. The legendary philosopher Lao Tzu asserts that a system of knots had been used as a script in ancient times.

The oldest characters, dating from the Shang period (2nd millennium B.C.) are to be seen on a stone found in 1930 and also on bones, bamboo tablets and early bronzes. As in Ancient Egypt, they were originally a symbolic, hieratic script, being written with a bamboo stylus in black paint.

From these symbols developed the so-called "seals". The Chancellery script came into use, corresponding to the change from the Ancient Egyptian Hieratic to the Demotic Script. When in later times paint-brushes made from the hair of the marten replaced hard bamboo styli, the Standard Script came into use, consisting of thick and thin brush-strokes. From the combination of about 214 "seal" characters with about 1,000 phonetic signs there gradually developed the 40,000 or so characters which a scholar was expected to know, compared with the mere 2,000 to 3,000 characters in common use.

This land of mighty elemental forces populated by peasants tied to the soil very soon gave birth to a basic philosophy which was to determine all later forms of religion and philosophy, even politics and sociology.

The Chinese sees the cosmos as "the great un-nameable", represented in the form of a circle, having no beginning and no end (Wu Ming). That which can be grasped and named is symbolised by a wavy line, which divides (Yu Ming) the circle (Wu Ki). The bright, positive or masculine half of the circle is the "Yang" principle, the dark, negative or feminine half is

Left: Emperor Tai-Kong of the Hsia dynasty out hunting.
Right page, top: high court officials and warriors of the Han period.
Bottom: fragment of a stele with inscriptions in the hieratic chancellery
script of the late Han.

the "Yin" principle. In each part there is the cell of its pole of its polar opposite, so that the diagram of the cosmos is like two mating fishes, each having one eye.

In later times this polarity of life was also symbolised by two lions, the "Yang Lion" having his paw on the globe, while the "Yin Lion" holds a tiger.

Two basic ideas are expressed here: the light and the globe tell of the great harmony, the deep inner accord of

The Shang dynasty. Below: a vassal prince performs the kotow before Emperor Chung Tang.
Right: the Emperor Tang on a tour of inspection of his provinces.

Heaven, Earth and Man, the symphony of the Divine and the Earthly. The darkness and the symbolic tiger tell of the darker side of creation, the chaos, confusion, disorder. From its very earliest days Chinese culture has swung like a pendulum between harmony and chaos.

It was the Emperor's chief task to preserve this harmony, to guarantee this accord of Heaven, Earth and Man, accord of the state and society with the divine powers. If chaos broke out, whether inundation by flooding rivers, civil war, famine, natural catastrophes or foreign invaders, the Emperor had broken the compact with the heavenly powers and had to fall, so that another, better ruler might arise and change the chaos into harmony again.

Accordingly, in the oldest monotheist religion, Shang-Ti is the god and the Emperor, or "Ti", his earthly image, the "Son of Heaven". Into these basic ideas of a fundamentally very rational peasant people were blended in ancient times a certain amount of animism, some natural divinities, the ancestor-cult and the belief in the effects of the elements "Wind and Water" (Feng-Shui). Consequently Chinese culture is the only great culture to have not forms of religion embodying a faith, but rather those embodying a code of conduct expressed in ethical and philosophical systems, to have social systems but no churches, official control but no dogma, and indeed, at a later stage of its history it even absorbed the religious systems of foreign cultures: Buddhism from India, Christianity from the Near East and Europe and in modern times the philosophy of Marxism-Leninism. But it adapted all these systems in accordance with its own character.

The Emperor Wu, founder of the Chou dynasty, while on a journey enters his travelling Audience Tent.

Ever since the 12th century B.C. genuine historical events become easier to discern and to date, but only from 841 B.C. onwards does one have an exact chronology. From then on the chronology of the ancient Chinese historian Ssu-ma-Ch'ien's "Records of the Historian" agrees with the dates given by the "Annals of the Bamboo Books".

Thus one learns of the decay of the Shang dynasty and the rise of the Dukes of Chou, who finally defeated the imperial army at Muye (1050) and then became the new rulers.

Under the Chou dynasty the Empire expanded southwards over the Yangtze Kiang and engaged in long-drawn-out battles with Turkish tribes migrating on horseback from the West, Mongol hordes from the North and the Tais of the South. These frontier wars led the Chinese to expand their military organisation and equipment to match those of their opponents. The two-horse chariot was brought into use and "margraves" were appointed to hold down the hotly-disputed frontier areas.

The rulers of Chou, now raised to the imperial throne, regulated the succession by stipulating that from thenceforward the eldest son of the principal wife should be heir to the throne. Other sons were given princely titles and appropriate estates. The Chou dynasty strengthened their government by alliances with the most important families of the provinces and thus created a kind of system of feudal tenure which replaces the abolute monarchy of the Shang emperors.

The change from the Shang dynasty to that of the Chou took place in accordance with the ancient law of China, that is, an empire fallen into chaos demands the harmony of a new political order. Therefore the Chou Emperors gave the exploited and oppressed peasantry a more just taxation system and agrarian reform. An idea was born in 800 B.C. which recurs time and time again in Chinese history—the founding of collectives, of people's communes and village communities. In accordance with the plan put forward by the Chou Emperor the land was laid out in square units, each of which when divided up in the pattern formed by the Chinese sign for "water well" (two vertical brush-strokes crossed by two horizontal ones) would become a "commune" of the "well-field system". Those who farmed the eight fields surrounding the central one would cultivate the central field jointly and pass on its harvest to the state as taxes.

This reorganisation of farm boundaries required great mathematical skill, so an imperial minister composed a book of rules containing formulae for calculating areas and including such items as the rule of three, calculation of square roots, simple geometry, equations with several unknowns and what is known in the West as the "Pythagorean Theorem".

A rich culture grew up. The Chou Emperors built roads and canals, constructed river-embankments to control the "Yellow Dragon" when in flood and sent expeditions to the sources of the great rivers. Contact with the Turkish tribes attacking from the West, whose sphere of influence extended as far as Turkestan and Persia, together with the rise of the Tsin in western China, who bore the brunt of the ever more vital defensive battle against the Hsiung-nu or Huns, brought all kinds of new, foreign, influences to bear on the Middle Kingdom. In those days, when, far to the West, Rome was founded, and the sage Thales initiated Greek philos-

14

Below: an Emperor of the Chou dynasty taking tea in the ladies'
apartments of his palace.

ophy, the Chinese adopted the ox-drawn plow from Asia Minor, the custom of burying the dead in coffins as in Egypt and introduced many previously unknown wares from the Middle East. Thus, for example, one finds Egyptian beads in Chinese graves. From India the Chinese learned certain cosmological and geographical ideas; from the Turks they borrowed the idea of the cavalry arm, mounted archers, trousers, shoes, stirrups, saddles and bridles as items of military equipment. Caps, belt-buckles and engraved Scythian longswords made their appearance; from the Greek sphere of influence they imitated the ornamental meander pattern, "leaping dogs" or wave pattern. Asia Minor provided the prototypes of the first copper coins.

Despite this significant cultural progress and social reforms, the Chou empire only weathered the storms of history for a short time. The main problems of the Chou dynasty were the ceaseless attacks of the Turkish and Hun tribes in the West, the conflict with the Tai peoples in the South and the empire's transformation into a feudal state. The "Western Chou Dynasty" came to an end as early as 770 B.C. But the longer-lived "Eastern Chou Dynasty" suffered from the increasing power of local chieftains, especially the mighty Tsin, to whom in the end the western half of the empire had to be abandoned.

Fragmentary states like the Han, Wei and Chao arose. In the "age of the warring kingdoms" (480–221 B.C.) the Chou empire disintegrated into a complex of warring feudal domains. In 225 the king of the Tsin deposed the last of the Chou dynasty and embarked on a process of establishing by means of lengthy local wars a new, centralist empire under the Tsin dynasty (221–206 B.C.). This new harmony, brought about by force of arms, succeeded the chaos and confusion of the feudal era.

In the Chou empire, despite magnificent cultural and social progress, political and human affairs had changed more and more from harmony to chaos, the effect of ceaseless attacks from outside and the passing of political power into the hands of local chieftains. Perhaps for that very reason the declining years of the Chou dynasty gave rise to China's greatest philosophers, who developed new systems of harmony.

Lao-Tzu (609–516 B.C. according to one source, 480–390 B.C. according to another) aimed to mould a type of human being, a new, perfect, rational man with whom one could build a harmonious society.

His sole work is the book "Tao-te-ching", the book of the eternal workings of reason, of the universal law which even human beings have to obey. Lao-Tzu turned away from the world, retired into solitude and taught his disciples the perfect workings of the divine spirit in the cosmos, nature, men's lives and morals—"Te". He said:

17

"I have three precious things
Which I hold on to and treasure,
Gentleness, moderation,
Aversion to the glamor of the
    world . . ."

In the course of time tradition created a popular Taoism, a mixture of speculation, breath-control, magic, mysticism, geomancy, together with a belief in ghosts and a personified, pantheistic natural philosophy. His disciples preached love, justice, respect, frugality and moderation as the features of true humanity.

But Lao-Tzu, like the almost contemporary Buddha of India, addressed the individual. Hermit that he was, his spiritual concern was focussed entirely on the individual, to whom he showed the lonely path to harmony.

Kung Fu-Tzu (551–479 B.C.), China's great pioneer of social ethics and political thinker, held different views. His concern was for social structure, the state, the regulation of human relationships—in brief, the formation of society.

Kung Fu-Tzu came from the little state of Lu on the Shantung peninsula. After lengthy study of ancient writings he became a government minister there and tried to put into practice his idea of a new ethic. When this attempt came to grief at the dissolute court of the local ruler, obsessed with war and rich living, Kung Fu-Tzu left Lu and set off on his long wanderings through dissension-torn China. These years of distress, poverty and powerlessness were the period of his most important teachings. He is said to have met the much older Lao-Tzu at this time.

A single work of his, the dry-as-dust "Annals of the State of Lu", has come down to us. His teachings were written down and formed into a system by his disciples.

Lao-Tzu's "Tao"—universal reason—was for Kung Fu-Tzu not merely a law of the cosmos but a moral code. "Te"—right action in accordance with "Tao"—he saw as virtue.

His concern was for the harmony of human order. On the basis of the ancient Chinese principle of veneration for ancestors the extended family became the nucleus of all his tenets. His maxims of right conduct are guidelines for the "five-fold relationships": that between prince and subject, father and son, older and younger brother, husband and wife and finally friend and friend.

In clear, rational propositions he defined almost all possible forms of conduct of one human being towards another, explained the necessity of politeness, belief in authority and obedience and the moral obligation to hold to the traditional order of things.

When his disciple Li asked him about the religious bases of his system, he answered: "Oh Li! How can I, who am only just beginning to understand mankind, know anything of the gods?" Confucianism as continued and extended by such great philosophers as Mo Ti (479–381), Lieh Yü-k'ou or, even more important, Meng K'o (372–289 B.C.), is indeed not a religion at all but an ethical system and social doctrine. Throughout all the centuries to the present day it has deeply influenced the Chinese mind at both individual and state level.

To Kung Fu-Tzu can also be ascribed the collection of China's Canonical Books (San-King), which have subsequently become a national heritage. They comprise the "Shi-King" or Book of Songs, the "Shu-King" or Book of Documents, the "I-King" or Book of Transformations (a collection

19

*Top: the birth of Kung Fu-Tzu. The legendary Dragon of Heaven appears
to his mother.*
*Bottom: Kung Fu-Tzu, as minister of Lu, orders rice to be distributed
to the poor.*

of oracles and prophecies), the "Li-Ki" or Notes on Ritual and finally Kung Fu-Tzu's own "Springs and Autumns (i.e. Annals) of the State of Lu".

To these five Canonical Books should be added the four classical writings of the Confucian School: the "Ta-Huo" (Great Doctrine of the Ancients), the "Lun Yü" (Teachings of the Master), the "Chung-Yung" (Holding to the Middle Way) and the writings of Meng K'o, who translated Kung Fu-Tzu's doctrines into popular idiom.

Thus it was Lao-Tzu with his appeal to universal reason, Tao concept and doctrine of self-formation, and Kung Fu-Tzu with his codification of human conduct and social relationships who from thenceforward showed the way to China's inner order. Both systems express the age-old Chinese aspiration to move from chaos to harmony.

2 Unity and Decay: from the Tsin Dynasty to the Han

From the "age of the warring states" (403–221 B.C.) and centuries-long decline of the Chou dynasty the Prince of Tsin emerged as victor.

The Tsin tribes, who had up to then been mainly responsible for the defense of China north-west of the Yangtze Kiang against the invading Inner-Mongolian horsemen, had a great deal of Hun, Turkish and Tibetan blood and were extremely warlike. Their chieftain Shih was the first to take the title "huang-ti" or "Sublime Emperor". The state which had previously been designated the "Middle Kingdom" was now called the Empire of the Tsin or Ch'in, in brief, "China". Emperor Shih Huang Ti (221–210 B.C.), ruling at a time when, far to the West, Hannibal fought against Rome and Carthage nevertheless suffered defeat, began a new epoch in the history of China. Just as in the West the Roman Empire arose, so Shih Huang Ti in the East made his empire a centralist state. He suppressed the nobility and the feudal system and turned China into a totalitarian state governed by thousands of laws. Chien-Yang became the capital, and from there the Emperor and his ministers governed the 36 provinces, which again were divided into prefectures.

Harmony and order returned with overwhelming force. Banditry was put down, new roads and canals were built, irrigation dams ensured the irrigation of the terraced fields, commerce revived and extended as far as distant lands.

Everything was regulated, everything was decided by the administration. Even the "seal script" or "chancellery script" was converted into the newer, more convenient form of the standard script called "kaishu", which has endured, with only minor changes, to the present day. Weights,

measures and even the gauge of wagon-wheels were standardised.

The people ruled over by the Tsin emperors were living in a world of myths and demons and imbued with Taoism and veneration of ancestors. But the Tsin dynasty put Confucianism, under the Chou dynasty merely discussed in theory, into practice.

Master Kung provided the idea of a state for the new centralist empire: regulation, standardisation, tight control by a well-organised political system based now on officials rather than on feudal loyalties.

Even before the Tsin came to power political philosophers such as Hsun-Tsu (305–235) developed the neo-Confucian principles deriving order from education and training, in brief, from regulated culture. Hsun-Tsu said: "The nature of man is evil, good is achieved only by culture . . . Man needs rules of right conduct and of justice. Only through education can a good society come about . . ."

A prince of the house of Tsin, Shang Yang, was given the task of working out the new state system. His disciple Li Ssu, as chancellor of Emperor Shih Huang Ti, put the new system into effect.

Its provisions included the rewarding of military and administrative success by a strictly defined system of promotions. Li Ssu controlled the use of all types of labor in accordance with a detailed "production plan". Only those who did truly "productive" work, for example in agriculture, the silk industry, manufacturing or in a craft, were granted civil rights. Exploiters and "parasites" such as merchants, artists, innkeepers, bankers and "capitalists", were ruthlessly pressed into service as manual laborers in the construction of canals, fortifications and public buildings and in drainage schemes. The state allocated land, servants, labor, even concubines and clothing.

Hegel's observation that China always comprises both the present and the past simultaneously, rings true. For much of what was put into practice in the Tsin state has been repeated in a new form two thousand years later, when Mao Tse-tung seized power as a "Red Huang Ti".

In the preface to Mao's works Lin Piao writes these words, which might well have come from Shang Yang or Li Ssu: "Study the writings of Mao, follow his doctrines and act in strict accordance with his rules".

Amongst these Tsin rules are some, such as those of Minister Sun-Tzu, which read like the Chinese counterpart of Machiavelli. Thus Sun Tzu lays down the following principle for the conduct of war against foreign powers:

"1. Undermine everything that is good in the land of your enemies.
2. Implicate the ruling class of your enemies in corruption and turn their youth into drug addicts.
3. Undermine the standing of all leaders by frequent scandals.
4. Do not hesitate to use the lowest and most repulsive creatures as collaborators.
5. Use all means in your power to impede the activity of the government.
6. Spread sectional disputes in the land of your enemies.
7. Incite the young to struggle against the old.
8. Devalue the traditions of your enemies, destroy all authority.
9. Organise sabotage and withdrawal of labor.
10. Sap the fighting spirit of the enemy by sensual desires and soft music.

posed on those who fail to
denounce a crime!

3. Reward merit with medals and
promotions but punish all critic-
ism of the state.

4. Dissolve close family relationships
by forbidding father and son to
dwell in the same kang. Send the
sons to labor on public works,
building dams, canals, roads and
fortifications.

5. In every province mingle each tribe
and people with the others."

11. Make the enemy believe in total
sexual freedom, turn his women
into whores.

12. Buy the services of traitors and in-
filtrate the enemy state with
spies."

Just as there were now instructions
as to how enemy provinces or states
could be made ripe for conquest (instructions which strongly resemble
those given in Kautilya's "Arthaka-
thastra", written in India in 300 B.C.),
so Kung Fu-Tzu's doctrines also provided rules for the inner life of the state
and society. Prince Shang Yang studied
Kung Fu-Tzu well, but where Master
Kung recommended "rule by kindness", Prince Shang Yang was all for
"rule by skilfully-based power". This
finds expression in the principles of
government formulated by Shang
Yang's disciple, Chancellor Li-Ssu:

"1. Divide and rule! Therefore divide
the whole nation into groups of
five and ten with instructions to
keep one another under surveil-
lance. Each house, each street is to
have a supervisor, each village a
local leader. Collective responsi-
bility is to fall on everyone's
shoulders!

2. The death penalty must be im-

The system introduced by Emperor
Shih Huang Ti and his chancellor Li
Ssu lay like a vast network of compul-
sion over China. All property became
"people's property" or rather "state
property". Life was hedged about by
rules, regulations and laws. The masses were disarmed, intermingled, in-
cessantly bombarded with propaganda and conscripted at will to labor
on public works, which the Tsin empire, like all dictatorships, indulged in
on a monumental scale.

Within a few years were built vast
flood-control embankments on the
Hwang-Ho and the Yangtze Kiang,
navigable inland canals and, most important of all, the gigantic Mongol
Wall, prototype of the Great Wall of
China, using the slave-labor of millions.

This, the largest work built by man,
stretches for 2,300 miles from the sea
up into the mountains, through river
valleys and over plains deep into western China. Large numbers of Chinese
were buried under its high walls, but in
less than eight years China was provided with a defensive wall against the
incursions of the Huns and Mongols.
The Great Wall, completed by the
Ming emperors in the sixteenth century, had a marked effect on the history of China. Constructed when

24

Below: the Great Wall was built during the Tsin period as a line of defense (dike with palisade) against the Mongols. Its transformation into the wall took place in the Ming period.

A Han woodcut showing a warrior with subjugated Hun princes.

Rome was building its empire on the ruins of Carthage and Greece, this fortification was to be the dam which would stem the onrush of the Central Asiatic nomadic peoples and provide the base from which the Chinese armies would push the invading Huns back to the West. Climatic changes in Northern Siberia and famine in Central Asia set off the great westward movement of the Hun hordes—the East being barred to them—and, six hundred years after the building of the wall, would initiate the Great Migration whose collision with the Roman Empire would bring the latter down in ruin.

This total nationalisation of life, this universal imperial rule of the Tsin was, in the end, not even able to tolerate the works of that Confucianism to which they owed their very existence. In 213 B.C. the Emperor decreed the burning of books. Scholars who interpreted Master Kung's precepts in a different, more humane manner were buried alive. The only exceptions to this destruction of the traditional spirit were, by order of Chancellor Li Ssu, those books which were of a practical or useful nature, those on agriculture, medicine and divination.

Shih Huang Ti, tyrant and emperor, died at the age of 49. His son Erh Shih Huang Ti ruled for only three years. He was a weakling. His own system defeated him, when high officials, court eunuchs and generals rose in rebellion. He was murdered in 207 B.C., and the local chieftains wielded more and more power.

The leader of the Han emerged victorious from the wars which attended the fall of the Tsin dynasty and in 202 B.C. ascended the imperial throne as Emperor Kao Tsu (206–195 B.C.). The great Han dynasty had entered the stage of history.

A violent palace revolution of the Han period.

Emperor Kao Tsu won the hearts of his people by kindness. He abolished the severe laws then in force except those punishing robbery, murder and bodily injury and began a certain degree of democratisation. He came from humble origins and was an ardent Confucian. Therefore he made no changes in the spirit of the centralist state but did away with the hardships and slavery suffered by the people. His own imperial authority he left undiminished. Under his influence the regulation of the Chinese state was carried out by a well-devised civil service. Imitating the Indian word for scholar, "mantrin", the well-educated, carefully-selected official was known as a "mandarin". All the privileges of the nobility and the great feudal vassals were swept away when the Emperor introduced his new hierarchy of officials. Everyone was given access to schools, everyone was given the op-

A violent palace revolution of the Han period.

portunity of advancing from rank to rank up the ladder of examinations. Education, talent and knowledge alone decided the fortunes of officers of state, reather than origin, family or high connections.

In the centuries that followed the Chinese mandarin system developed. According to rank mandarins were allowed clothes of certain colors, embroidered figures (herons, teal, panthers etc.) and buttons of certain materials (turquoise, coral, gold, crystal etc.) on their black satin caps.

Candidates for state examinations had to undergo written examinations in history, statecraft, administration, knowledge of the five Canonical Books and the canon of the four classical writings of Confucianism in strict seclusion. The higher the rank the harder the examination became, being assessed on the beauty of calligraphy and copiousness of quotations. To this were added the doctrines of Taoism, ranging from asceticism, breath control, medicinal lore and comprehension of natural forces to magic and geomancy. The doctrines of the Neo-Pythagoreans and Essenes from Greece and the Middle East and Yoga doctrines from India reached China by western and southern trade routes.

Under the Han Emperor Wu Ti (140–87 B.C.) China entered one of the Golden Ages of its history. In masterly campaigns the army broke the power of the Huns, operating from the Great Wall and waging war on the nomads in the plains and mountain valleys on the far side of it. For the first time in history military rockets were used. For a long time China had possessed many kinds of explosive and propellant powders, which had till then only been used at festivities and for the purpose of driving away demons.

As the routes to the West became safer, the Han Empire embarked on the task of building the "Silk Road".

Beginning at the "Nephri Gate" near the marches of the salt lake Lop Nor, the southern Silk Road ran across the Tarim basin to Tashkent and Ferghana in Bactria, whilst the northern branch ran via Hami and Kucha to Kashgar. These long caravan and post-roads, which crossed Persia and ended at the eastern shores of the Mediterranean, were provided with military posts, guest-houses, wells and food-depots. The western provinces Kansu and Southern Turkestan were first defended by army camps and then systematically opened up to Chinese settlers. Embassies were sent off to India, to the Hellenistic parts of Persia and to the Scythians.

The Imperial Court at Sian grew into a city with an immensely active cultural life, where scholars, men of letters, artists and statesmen gathered. A state academy, T'ai Huo, devised complicated syllabi for the training of civil servants and ordained that the highest rank be "po chi", or Doctor. The emperors introduced the ritual of heavenly sacrifices, which the ruler of China, with his people and court, was to offer every year to the powers of heaven and earth as a token of the constant renewal of the harmony between the Divine and the Human, the Eternal and the Earthly. From thenceforward on this occasion each new year was given its own individual name.

Ocean-going Chinese junks sailed along the coasts to the Sunda Islands, India and even as far as Ceylon, where they bartered gold and silks for glass and pearls and established trading relationships with Graeco-Roman mariners who, crossing the Indian Ocean by the "Nearchos Route", also made land in Ceylon.

Under Wu Ti the empire occupied twice its area at the beginning of the Han dynasty, and it is an expression of its national self-confidence that the famous "Shi Ki" ("Records of the Historian") and the bibliography of the Imperial Library were written about this time.

World-wide trade-relations with the Indian, Iranian and Graeco-Roman spheres of influence brought not only grapes, pomegranates, saffron, beans, incense and nut-trees from the Middle East to the gardens of China, intellectual influences were also everywhere evident. Splendid engraved plates of silver and bronze clearly show Greek and Indian influence, human and animal figures indicate models which must have come from distant lands. Later finds of bronzes, filigree work, nephrite plates, lacquer bowls and coins prove a high level of artistic creativity. On the Greek and Indian model poems, epic sagas and dramas based on the campaigns against the Huns were written.

No human system lasts for ever, none can flourish indefinitely. So it was with the Han dynasty.

Chaos once again destroyed harmony—a distressingly frequent occurrence in Chinese history. A regent, Wang Mang, brought back the outmoded ways of the Chou period, with its aristocracy and feudal system, and thus wrought havoc with the hitherto excellent administrative system. Money lost its value because of false coinages containing copper and tin, as in the late Roman Empire, inflation weakened the economy. Once again the peoples of Central Asia, the Huns at their head, invaded the border provinces and uprooted Chinese settlers.

A rebellion by the "Red Eyebrows" swept away the incompetent government and restored the empire. After

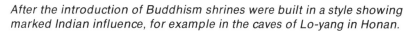

the sack of the capital, Ch'ang-an, a descendant of the eastern Han clan, the Emperor Liu Siu (25–27 A.D.) ascended the throne in the new capital, Lo-yang. The age of the "Eastern Han" was beginning. The people, weary of wars and rebellions, returned to law and order. The Empire, fossilised in its vast civil service, regulations and rationalism, armed itself with a new religion which filled the gap left by Kung Fu-Tzu in the field of metaphysics. Even in China man cannot live on bread alone. The ancient veneration of ancestors, belief in demons and magic-working Taoism no longer satisfied the intellectual and spiritual needs of the upper ranks of society.

Thus it was that Buddhism, coming in from India via Tibet, quickly spread, exerting an immense influence on the philosophical, religious and artistic development of China.

Buddhism, which in India and Tibet at this time had absorbed many elements of Hinduism and the worship of the gods of Central Asia, reached China in its "Mahayana" form—the "great ship" of salvation. Many myths and a large number of religious mysteries go to form this ship. But the helmsman of the "Mahayana" is still the "Enlightened One", who steers the course of asceticism, deliverance from self and interior silence.

Under the Emperor Ming Ti (55–75 A.D.) a Chinese mandarin travelled to India and brought back to China the Pali Canon, the gospel of primitive Buddhism.

A new Golden Age began. Chinese commercial enterprises and indeed Chinese towns were set up as far away as Indo-China and Malaysia. Pan Shao's expedition reached the Persian Gulf and Antioch. In the time of Trajan and Hadrian Chinese trading junks cautiously worked their way through the Red Sea and Necho's canal to Alexandria, Antioch, even Syracuse in Sicily. Under the Roman Emperor Antoninus Pius (circa 145) a Chinese reconnaissance expedition appeared on the fringes of the Caucasus. At this time Chinese power in Central Asia reached a new peak.

It was then that the Huns began their long march to the West, which was to set off the Great Migration.

In Lo-yang about the year 105 A.D. the mandarin Ts'ai Lun invented a process for making paper, to save the expense of costly pieces of silk previously used for writing. The first glazed tiles made their appearance, and the age of "proto-porcelain" began. Both these skills, paper-making and the art of azulejo glazing, the Emperor's Turkish bodyguard took with them into exile in Western Turkestan, to Samarkand, Bokhana, Merv and Kashgar. In the seventh century A.D., when the Arabs invaded these provinces, Arab travellers brought these inventions from the Middle East via Egypt and North Africa to Moorish Spain, and from there they were disseminated to the rest of Europe.

Philosophy and literature flourished once again, a dictionary of characters was issued, canonical writings incised in stone tablets made it possible to obtain a print and thus prepared the way for the later art of block printing. The monastery of Hu Chang Sse was the center of Buddhist learning. Lo-yang was adorned with wooden temples and colored wall-reliefs.

Soon there were new Hun incursions, mutinies among the troops guarding the frontiers, even a popular uprising, that of the "Yellow Turbans". Harmony declined, the chaos of conflicting generals and governors inundated the dying Han dynasty. In 220 A.D., the last Han Emperor

Buddhist paintings: right, the monk Ti-Tsang; left, the Bodhisattva Kuan-Yin.

handed over the seal of state to a victorious general.

There followed centuries of disintegration. The great empire split up into a large number of small states. It sank into a chaos of unceasing struggles for power, fought by provinces, tribes and generals one against the other.

Right: scene from the court at Lo-yang.

3 The Threshold of the Middle Ages: the Sui and T'ang Dynasties

China was constantly being invaded by foreign peoples from the West. Under Liu Pei, a descendant of the Han, the state of Shu was created in the South-West in opposition to the state of Wei in the North and North-West. When it was attacked, its ruler moved 10,000 Chinese families from Yunnan into the province of Szechwan. A third state arose, that of Wu in Central and South-East China, having "Lien-Ye" (Nanking) as its capital. This period is known as the "Age of the Three Kingdoms".

In the state of Wu, during the reign of Sun Hao in 264, tea was mentioned for the first time, as a drink coming from the southern mountains. From Wu the Chinese national drink had spread by the eighth to tenth century to the North and reached Japan about 750 A.D.

The outcome of the wars between the Three Kingdoms was a new but short-lived Tsin dynasty. Under these rulers, whose capital was once again at Lo-yang, great counter-attacks were launched from the now repaired Great Wall against the Hsiung-nu or Huns. The latter finally gave up in despair and set out determinedly westwards. They were pushed back to the Caspian Sea and circa 375 A.D. sparked off the Great Migration in Europe.

The Tsin kings of Lo-yang fell victim to the eunuchs and the hareem of their court. When an invading T'opa horde from the West stormed Lo-yang in 311, the richly-adorned wooden temples and palaces of the city burned in a huge conflagration. In the flames was lost the great library containing irreplaceable and unique manuscripts from ancient times.

After the fall of the Tsin the empire broke up completely. North of the Yangtze Kiang alone there sprang up three Chinese and 13 barbarian states.

the West, which also arose from the ruins of tribal wars, migrations and fragmentation into small states and attempted to restore a great vanished imperium. And just as in the Carolingian West, China's T'ang period saw economy, culture and art flourish to an unsurpassed degree right into the Middle Ages of its history. Under the T'ang the "Middle Kingdom" became for the first time a true world power.

But even the now departed period of decay had its highlights. In the days of the "Warring Kingdoms" and even more so in the subsequent period of decay and confusion, many people turned away from a world gone mad. Never before had there been so many hermits, monks and scholar-poets in China as in the century following the end of the Han dynasty. China's "Age of Religion" coincided with the centuries of political confusion and fragmentation. Large numbers of Chinese monks made pilgrimages to India, Tibet and the border provinces of Persia and returned with new Buddhist or Hindu writings to give these religions new impetus. In this way the ideas of Hellenistic Ghandara, and Persia and India's rich store of astronomical, mathematical and medical knowledge found their way to Chinese Buddhist monasteries in caves or on mountain-tops. Belief in the transmigration of souls, in reward or punishment for one's deeds in the after-life and in rebirth seeped down into China's consciousness. Learned pilgrims like Fa Hsien, translator of the Indian Sutras, wrote the memoirs of their long travels among strange peoples.

When public life is as dissatisfying as in the strife-torn petty states of the age of decline, the active mind of China always applies itself to new works of art and learning. About 436 the scholar Ts'ien Lo-tse reported the

This profusion of small states lasted from 317 until 589.

In the meantime South of the Yangtze Kiang the empire of the "Eastern Tsin" came into being from 317 to 420, having Nanking as its capital. The tangled history of these years is an uninterrupted series of wars, tribal disputes, treason, murder and intrigue. Even the Taoist and Buddhist sects came to blows, and both fought the Confucians. The vast land was plagued with slaughter, destruction and catastrophe until finally in 588–589 one of the "five southern dynasties" produced a general called Yang Chien, of the house of Sui. With the aid of a massive revolt of the peasantry he succeeded in uniting the various petty states and in restoring the empire.

A new harmony was established, the Sui period became an epoch of vast expansion of power and an upsurge of political, economic and cultural achievement lasting until well into the great T'ang period (618–906 A.D.).

Chronologically and historically the T'ang corresponds roughly to the beginning of Charlemagne's empire in

construction of an armillary sphere for determining the positions of the stars. About the same time the botanist Hi Han invented a taxonomy of the plant world, and the tradition of historical writing was continued with great accuracy by a large number of diligent mandarins. A significant example of the practical viewpoint of the Chinese is Tu Y, who invented the water-mill and a primitive irrigation pump but was also the author of commentaries on ancient chronicles. A cartographer called P'ei Siu drew the first maps of the Middle Kingdom. An age of great

calligraphers and watercolorists began. The artists chose as their subject-matter the harmony of sky, landscape, plants and men.

One of the poets of the age was T'ao Yüan Ming, born of a poor peasant family, who lived as a mandarin of subordinate rank at the imperial court at Nanking surrounded by a corruption only thinly veiled by Confucian aphorisms. Disgusted by what he had seen, he returned home, cultivated his land with his own hands and devoted his evenings to philosophy and poetry. He became the "Anacreon of China",

seeking forgetfulness in intoxication. To him, "Master of the Five Meadows", people made pilgrimages from all over China to hear his songs praising the simple life:

"Even as a boy I was not like
    the common herd—
in my heart I loved the mountains.
But I fell into ways of error,
    was ensnared in filth,
and the world held me in thrall
    for thirty years...
The bird of passage longs
    for its woodland home,

35

the fish in the pond
can never forget the lake . . ."

Once again China's soul, in its painting, philosophy and poetry, sought the harmony at the heart of creation.

Against this scene of the decay and brilliance of the "Warring Kingdoms" there stands out the Jade Palace built for a collateral line of the imperial family in Nanking. The delightful park of the "Hill of Flamingo Clouds" is covered with Stupas, which the Chinese were then beginning to build in imitation of Indian Buddhist models. Gaily-colored wooden pagodas were built as shrines to Buddha.

From the Indian Stupa developed the bell-shaped temple housing relics with graceful, open places of sacrifice outside a massive Stupa. The pagoda, however, took the shape of a tower with curved tiled roofs, dragons as gargoyles and invariably an odd number of floors.

In the imperial palaces the guardians of these temples were animals, legendary creatures and weird figures of heroes and demons made of stone and bronze.

In imitation of the "Thousand Buddha Caves" of Tunhuang on the Silk Road at the side of the Tarim basin, the grotto temples of Yünkang (Shansi) and the cave temples of Oyang were built.

Longing for harmony between the divine and the human, for oneness of the soul with nature also inspired painters working in watercolors on silk or paper scrolls. For them harmony was the greatest good, and so they write for every "Kakimono picture" a certain number of appropriate 'ko verses':

"The rain falls on the
Yangtse Kiang.

The water lilies are like
delicate scissor-cuts.
The splendor of the Six Dynasties
passes like a dream!
Nothing remains but the
plaintive song of the birds.
Thankless are the green
willow-trees,
which cast their shadows
over the terraced city.
They will come into leaf again
as they did long ago
on the Ten Mile Dyke and sway
in the mist . . ."
(Anonymous, circa 500 A.D.)

And in very truth this longing was fulfilled. Out of the mists of century-long chaos and haze of apparent downfall there rose one day the blazing sun of a new beginning. In 588–589 A.D. one of the rival generals, Yang Chien of the house of Siu, outdid all his competitors. He entered the "Hill of Purple and Gold" in Nanking as victor and as emperor took the name Wen Ti (580–604 A.D.). The great land of China was ripe for reunification once again as the "Middle Kingdom". The longing of the peasantry for peace and order, the national aspirations to greatness and mastery over chaos prepared the way for Wen Ti's army of liberation into all the petty states and barbarian domains. With amazing speed he succeeded in toppling all the petty dynasties, and within two decades restored the old Han Empire as a centralist state with Nanking as its capital.

The Emperor Wen Ti was not an outstanding personality. Good fortune decreed that he should make his appearance at exactly the right time and provided him with the right mixture of cunning and strength to bring about what millions of people had been desiring for a long time—the unification of the Chinese Empire.

Art and scholarship derived no benefit from the appearance of the new Emperor. His task was solely the creation of unity and a basis for future development.

Wen Ti successfully reformed the legal and administrative system. He re-introduced the sophisticated examination system which decided the selection and promotion of officials.

In the meantime his armies recaptured all the lost provinces as far as Indo-China, Turkestan and the Korean frontier.

The tough, cunning Emperor was so immersed in his work of restoration that he failed to perceive that his second son, Yang Kuang, was impatiently ambitious for power. A conspiracy was hatched in the restored imperial palace at Loyang, and open rebellion broke out. The emperor was assassinated by the rebels, and his son ascended the throne as Emperor Yang Ti (605–618 A.D.).

The new Emperor had sufficient intelligence to execute his accomplices in parricide and to disassociate himself from the deeds of violence which had been committed. However, the people never forgave him his betrayal of the former Emperor and called him "Emperor Yang the Cruel". The fortune won by the sword proved fickle to the new Emperor. First his campaign against Korea was a failure, then he was defeated by the Turks. The people rose in revolt, and he was murdered.

Once again it was a general who put down the rising chaos. Li Shih-Min bribed the Turkish regiments, and with their help deposed the Sui dynasty. Then he placed his father Li Yüan on the imperial throne.

Li Yüan was of the family of the Princes of T'ang, and with him began the T'ang Dynasty (618–906 A.D.)

The Emperor T'ai Tsung gives audience, his decrees being written down immediately in the Imperial Chancellery (T'ang dynasty).

after only 28 years of Sui rule. As emperor Li Yüan took the name Kao Tsu (618–626 A.D.).

The old gentleman entirely lacked any strength or power of decision, and merely acted as figurehead. The helmsman was his energetic son, General Li Shih-Min, who secured the unity of China by means of a series of campaigns. After his father's death he ascended the throne as the Emperor T'ai Tsung (627–649) in the rebuilt capital, Ch'ang-an.

He had come to power with the aid of the Turkish regiments. But he was aware of the danger threatened by this "Praetorian Guard", and it was one of his acts of State to exile the Turkish corps, together with their families, to the furthest end of the empire—Turkestan. These Turks took with them the knowledge of paper and porcelain-making, rocket-making, glazes and bronze-founding. Characteristically Chinese features such as the crescents, adorned with horse-tails, of their military bands, the political influence of the harem, the state school for pages and the rank-system for army officers and civil servants, went with the exiled Turks to the fringes of the Middle East and of Europe, where, through the Arab conquest of the eighth century and the westward movement of the Turks in the 12th–13th centuries, they lived on in other cultures.

Emperor T'ai Tsung became one of the most significant rulers of the new world power. He divided the vast empire into 10 (later 15) military provinces and organised the government of the country from the center through governors dependent on Ch'ang-an. His fame spread to India and Persia. He concluded a treaty with Tibet and consolidated it by marrying a Tibetan princess. That remote highland region now came entirely under Chinese cultural influence. The warlike Uigurs in the South-West also became subjects of the "Middle Kingdom". From Japan came the embassy of Prince Shotoku Tai Ishi to study the political, religious and cultural situation in China. When they returned to Japan they brought home not only knowledge of paper-making, porcelain, tea cultivation, silk farming, horses and many new varieties of fruit, but also the principles for the renewal of Japan through the "Taikwa Reform". So powerful was the new emperor's position that in 643 there arrived an embassy from the Patriarch of "Fu Lin" (the Chinese term for Constantinople) to initiate formal relations.

The Emperor's son, Kao Tsung (650–683) continued the pattern of conquest and advanced the frontiers of

Aristocratic society gathers in the courtyard of the imperial palace and is entertained with feats of arms. T'ang period.

China to Iran. North Korea and Manchuria were annexed to the empire. The widow of this Emperor excluded her own son from the succession and reigned for twenty years with the aid of her mandarins and eunuchs, moving the capital back to Lo-yang.

Under the Emperor Hsüan Tsung (713–756) the T'ang dynasty reached its second zenith. Initially an extremely wise and virtuous ruler, the latter came in later years very much under the influence of a lady of the harem, Yuang Kuei Fei, beautiful but much given to intrigue. A dramatic love story took place at the court at Lo-yang, which in Chinese literature has provided a theme for numerous poems, novels and plays. In 755 the beautiful Yang Kuei Fei was executed after a palace revolution. The emperor was powerless to prevent it. For the first time the dynasty tottered. Discontent with the unharmonious state of affairs caused by the "Son of Heaven's" way of life spread widely, and in his later years Emperor Hsüan Tsung was not only embroiled in love-affairs, he also left too much power in the hands of his mandarins, eunuchs and generals. When he took stern measures against the lethargy and indolence of the numerous Buddhist monks and intervened in the dissension between the latter and the strict Confucians, he made many enemies for himself amongst the religious-minded.

Finally a Turkish military governor rebelled, foreign peoples, such as the Uigurs, the Khitan and the Tibetans invaded the country. Bands of rebel peasants roamed the land. The lovely cities of Lo-yang and Ch'ang-an were looted by troops and rebels. The Emperor abdicated in favor of his son. Despite these unfortunate developments his reign was a "golden age of art and poetry". Under Hsüan Tsung

the T'ang Empire reached its highest level of cultural achievement. However, from a peak all roads run downhill. After a series of weak rulers China entered into a decline, and the unity of the empire began to suffer. This took place around 850 A.D., at a time when in the West Charlemagne's empire was disintegrating under the rule of his sons. Around 874 a peasants' uprising raged in a state which had lost harmony and was sliding into chaos. Significantly, the revolt was led by a peasant and a scholar. In 879 Canton was stormed, plundered and almost totally destroyed.

About the time when in Europe the last Carolingians were handing over authority to more powerful local lords and tribal kings, in China the last T'ang emperor, Chao Süan Ti, decided to pass the imperial power to a local ruler. The empire split into two halves, the eastern one having Kaifeng as its capital, the western one Lo-yang. Ch'ang-an, destroyed and now rebuilt, was renamed "Ta An" ("Great Peace").

The fields of "Great Peace" were haunted by memories of the once mighty T'ang. The game of Empire was lost.

The Sui Dynasty had been distinguished by many great public works: the "Imperial Calan" between the Yangtze and the Hwang Ho had been restored and widened, the Great Wall had been repaired and lengthened, in the various capital cities magnificent buildings had been put up. These events are all recorded in the "Sui Shu", the great chronicle of the Sui period. The two T'ang annals, "Kiu Shu" and "Sin T'ang Shu", report even more splendid cultural achievements.

The T'ang period was more than anything else an age of active religious

life. Buddhism was enriched by the esoteric Hindu Tantras and absorbed aspects of magic from Tibet.

Like the monastic movement of Cluny in the West, China's monastery school of Vinaya was founded to foster monastic discipline, asceticism and control of the will, while the second monastic school, Dhyana (which gave rise to the Japanese Zen) promoted cultivation, meditation and the intensification of the inner life. Questing pilgrims set out once again on long journeys, the best-known being those of the monk I Tsing, who travelled to India and Hüan Tsang, who walked to Tibet, Central Asia and Northern India.

About 635 the Persian Alopen brought Nestorian Christianity from his homeland to China. The fire and sun cult of Zoroaster penetrated the mountains and reached Szechuan and Sikiang In the seventh century the Muslim conquest of Turkestan brought Islam to Central China via the Tarim basin and the Silk Road.

But the T'ang's most significant achievements were in the fields of literature and poetry. In Lo-yang and Ch'ang-an learned academies were founded, the examination system was improved and extended. By order of the Emperors, leading mandarins wrote histories and commentaries on the contemporary state of knowledge. A large number of encyclopedias were composed. The first of general interest was written by Tu Yu (735–812), a second, dealing only with medicine and therapeutics, was written by a consortium of scholars at about the same time. The latter contains a full study of acupuncture, which was then already fully established. From 701–762 lived the greatest and most colorful lyric poet of Chinese literature —Li Po, known as the "Evening

Star". He was already a poet at ten years of age, then led a vagabond life, wandering through China's provinces with lyre and sword. As one of the "Six Idlers of the Bamboo Stream" the poet proved a talented drinker. In the end the Emperor offered him the highest offices in the land. Highspirited, constantly intoxicated yet producing a constant stream of masterly verses, he quickly became the center of a galaxy of artistic talent at the court of the Emperor Hsüan Tsung. But fate entangled him finally in the intrigues being hatched around the Emperor's beautiful beloved. He escaped by boat through lonely reed-fringed lakes and remote tributaries, ending his life as the guest of a relative in a distant province. He wrote powerful verses about loneliness and longing:

"O loneliness of the night hours,
   how sore you afflict me!
I blow out my candle and seek
   rest in sleep.
But alas! the moonlight full of
   longing
Creeps over to me and into my
   very bed . . ."

Finally at peace, he finds wisdom:

"As our life
is nothing but one long dream,
why then make haste and struggle
so important?"

Each of Li Po's poems is like one of the delicate watercolors of the Sui and T'ang periods, full of masterly simplicity and power of expression. Apart from this scroll-painting there were important Buddhist frescoes and other religious graphic art. One of the main themes of this kind of art was the Kuan Yin or the "Merciful Heavenly Mother" of the Bodhisattva.

The plastic art of the T'ang period attained worldwide fame. Produced in ceramics, stone and bronze, the most famous were the horse figurines. The names of the figurine-painter Kan Han (720–780) and the flower-painter and poet Pien Luen (circa 800) deserve especial mention as outstanding exponents of these Chinese arts.

The storms of history have removed all traces of the magnificent buildings of the T'ang period, for example the "Palace of the Immortals" in Lo-yang.

The Emperor Hsüan Tsung of the T'ang dynasty has poetry recited before him and orders the poems to be copied by his Court Scribes.

41

4 From the Sung Dynasty to the Mongol Invasion

After the decline of the T'ang dynasty China had to endure yet another period of chaos, during which Mongol-Turkish tribes set up petty states in large parts of the empire. Admittedly these foreigners were greatly influenced by China's higher culture and soon adopted Chinese ways in such matters as script, literature, and administrative organisation, but the unity of the empire was broken: there were finally five states in the North and about ten in the South.

But the period of confusion did not last for very long. In 960, only one lifetime after the end of the T'ang, the army raised a general, Chao Kwang-yin, to the throne. He founded the Sung dynasty.

His new empire consisted of no more than the Chinese heartlands. The peoples around the periphery maintained their forcible occupation of the frontier provinces, the connection with Central Asia and soon, too, with the South, where in 973 Annam became independent as the Kingdom of Tong-king (North Vietnam), was lost. On every side border states were being set up or already existed on what had been Chinese sovereign territory. Thus in 907 was founded the "Kingdom of the Khitan" by conquering Manchurian invaders. This kingdom included Manchuria, North Korea, parts of Mongolia and Chinese territory as far as the district of Tientsin. The mighty political unit was called by the Persians "Chytai", by the Mongols "Kitat", by the Arabs "Hitai" and in William of Rubruk's chronicle (1253) "Cathay". It is under this name that it appears in European reports. Columbus set off to look for "Cathay".

After the Khitan had conquered Peking and Kaifeng as well, they called their state "Liao", after one of their principal tribes.

When in 1123 the Khitan were finally defeated by another Tungus people, the Nü-chen, the northern state still posed a constant threat to the Sung empire established in Central and South China.

When the event took place and Kaifeng, the former capital of the Sung was captured, the precious imperial collections and, most important of all, the great libraries, were plundered and partly destroyed. This terrible loss for the student of cultural history was slightly compensated for in the field of literature by the fact that sometime before (circa 940) a scholar named Feng Tao had invented the art of printing from wooden tablets and thus some printed copies of the classics survived even in the South.

At the same time Nü-chen tribes founded the kingdom called "Kara Khitai" in Turkestan (1125).

The Tungus Nü-chen joined forces with other Mongolian groups and destroyed the Khitai kingdom in the North. The leader of the Nü-chen, Akuta, set himself up in Peking as emperor, naming his dynasty "Kin" (gold). By 1130 the Nü-chen and their Mongolian allies had reached the Yangtze Kiang. Mongol conquerors crushed North China, but the same happened to them as had happened to all foreign invaders: within three generations they had become Chinese in many ways. The higher culture absorbed the people of the steppe. Enjoying their conquests to the full, the new overlords degenerated. Other foreign peoples, such as the Mongols, Turks and Uigurs, set up petty states. The expropriated Chinese peasantry joined together in a front of national unity against the Nü-chen overlords. Their discontent and rebellion prepared the way for the future, even greater wave of conquest.

Whilst all around the Chinese heartland confusion, foreign domination and the setting up of independent border states grew worse and worse, the Sung dynasty ruled their truncated empire first from Kaifeng (as the "Northern Sung" until 1125) and then from Nanking (as the "Southern Sung" until 1279).

Even in the days of the Emperor Chen Tsung (998–1022) the Sungs had been obliged to pay the invading Khitan 200,000 ounces of silver and 300,000 bales of silk annually as tribute. Under the Emperor Jen Tsung in 1043 this payment was increased to a million ropes of coin (each of 1,000 coins), 100,000 bales of silk and 30,000 parcels of tea.

That, of course, was not only a humiliation for the former "Middle Kingdom" but also a heavy burden of taxation for its people. For this reason the Emperor Shen Tsung (1068 to 1085) made financial reforms, reducing government spending by 40%. A kind of "state capitalism" was based on models taken from the past (Chou or Tsin periods). The paid professional army was replaced by a people's army. Chancellor Wang An Shih (1021–1086) was the great reformer of the Sung states.

He fought against the spreading Neo-Confucianism, reformed the legislature and the civil service but was defeated in the end by the resistance of the court and the mandarins. When in 1125 the Nü-chen attacked and destroyed Kaifeng, the dynasty of the "Northern Sung" ended with the "Painter-Emperor" Hui Tsung.

In the South the "Southern Sung" dynasty managed to hold out for another 150 years with their capital at Nanking. But even they were described as "vassals" of the Nü-chen in state treaties. A large part of the riches pro-

The Emperor Chen Tsung receives the representatives of tributary provinces in the city of Kaifeng.

duced by the flourishing towns and villages of Southern China went in tribute to the "Kara K'itai" and the Nü-chen. The taxes collected by the Southern Sung circa 1189 from gold, silver and leadmining monopolies, from silk farms, porcelain factories, tea plantations, salt and paper production amounted to 65 million ropes of coin annually. In Southern and South-West Asia Chinese money acted as an international currency. Banks even began to issue paper money, which was backed by the reserves of gold and silver at Nanking.

The Sung empire can be described as rich and flourishing in many cultural and intellectual fields, but also as politically and militarily weak. It was ripe for the next mighty onrush from the steppes of Central Asia, an onrush which was to overthrow it.

In the last days of the Sung, exactly as in contemporary Europe, there arose a gentry class composed of important landowners and rich city merchants. It was this cultivated but also selfish stratum of society which groaned most loudly under the Sung Emperors' high taxation and attempts at "socialism". Their ambition was to be left in full enjoyment of their possessions and the income deriving from them, and it was consequently they who flirted with the new Mongol conquerors. From these foreigners, whom they sought to win over by good behavior, they hoped for the preservation of their social status. The China of the Sung could no longer resist the Mongol hordes.

Apart from its political and military weakness the Sung dynasty, surrounded by foreign states and foreign conquerors, was a moment of respite in the historical progress in which the Chinese heartlands attained a high level of culture. Trading junks found

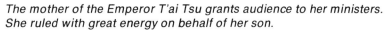

The mother of the Emperor T'ai Tsu grants audience to her ministers. She ruled with great energy on behalf of her son.

their way to the South Seas, to the Sunda Archipelago, to India, Arabia, East Africa and Sicily. Pilgrim groups of several hundred Chinese and Uigur monks went to Gandhara (in the Hellenistic East), to Maghadha and Nepal. Sanskrit texts were translated, Buddhist and Taoist monastery schools were founded. Academies for the mandarin examinations were set up in the towns. The "Neo-Confucian School" flourished. Scholars wrote a large number of learned works, including some on philosophy and medicine. Literature attained new heights through the publication of histories, lexicons, geographical works and encyclopedias. In one dictionary of the Chinese language 53,525 characters were listed, while a catalogue of antiquities and inscriptions demonstrates an interest in archaeology. As in the meantime the art of printing from wooden tablets had been discovered, many of the standard works became available to a large public.

The arts, too, were in a flourishing state. The shadow play was introduced, and in cave temples and richly-frescoed holy places, such as the funerary temple of the Emperor Hing Tsung, the sumptuous colors and forms of the religious imagination are given free play.

However, the most magnificent achievements were in the field of watercolor painting on silk or paper. In a thousand variations artists depict the "mountains and water" theme, the sublime solitude of nature in its harmony of sky, earth and water. Painting academies introduced "po hi", the school of bamboo painting, which had to be practised for twenty years before one could attempt a real picture.

Kuo Hsi (circa 1050) is China's most important landscape painter, but the Emperor Hui Tsung (circa 1125)

also painted "Pigeon on Peach Branch" and "Flowering West Garden". Chao Ch'ang is famous for his flower paintings, Chou Wen Shü for his portraits. Greatest of all, however, is the fame of the great horse-painter Li Lung Mien (circa 1100), reputed the greatest genius of Chinese painting.

Porcelain manufacture reached high standards in shape and beauty of the brownish or dark green glaze. Bronze-founding, ivory-carving, lacquer work and woodcarving flourished.

But all this brilliant culture, the impressive opulence of the cities and the refinements of their way of living were only a coating of paint covering up disaster. The empire was weak, its citizens demoralised, its defences paralysed. The abyss opened and discharged a flood of new, young and warlike peoples who in one overwhelming assault swept away all the magnificence of the late Sung. The Mongols were on the move.

The man known to history as Jenghiz Khan was originally called Temuchin and was the son of Jessugei Khan, chieftain of the Nujakin Mongols, whose tents were pitched by the Orchon. "The tribes on the Orchon, like all Mongols, dwell in black wagons and white tents. They live by hunting and off their herds, dress in skins and feed on meat and milk." In Mongolia war of all men against each other had always been the rule. The many Mongol tribes mangled each other in savage warfare. Knowing no law and no mercy, they destroyed all enemy life. For them women were only booty, young men merely slaves. Their warcries had been heard and had struck terror into their enemies since time immemorial in the stormy wind rushing down from the high peaks of the

Himalayas and Altai onto the plains of waving grass and the sandy gullies of the Gobi.

Out of this primitive world of ceaseless struggle arose a great man, Jenghiz Khan, who in lightning guerilla actions and merciless campaigns united unruly Central Asia with an iron hand. In the civilised world nobody took the slightest notice of the upheavals among the peoples of the Gobi Desert and the resulting unification of all the Mongols. But about 1200 Jenghis Khan achieved success: he became the Great Khan of hundreds of thousands of warlike Mongols, and the plains of Central Asia echoed with the thunder of millions of hooves.

He assembled a vast army of horsemen and led it to the borders of Persia and India and to the Volga. While his subordinate commanders prepared attacks on the Caliphate of Bagdad, the conquest of the remainder of Russia and the invasion of Europe, in 1215 the Great Khan led his immense army to Northern China, into the kingdom of their cousins, the Nüchen.

The attack on the Chinese cultural sphere began.

The conquest took place in several waves. Jenghiz Khan himself died in 1227, but his heirs continued the world war. Mongko Khan and then Kublai Khan succeeded to the leadership.

The Mongol commanders quickly learned the art of capturing walled towns and fortresses. The citizens, merchants, craftsmen, officials and artists of the Chinese cities, as well as the masses of peasantry who had taken refuge within their walls, thought themselves safe as long as there were soldiers on the walls to tear gaps in the ranks of the advancing horsemen by

hurling rocks, pots of burning naphtha, blazing spears and firing rockets. But then the fortresses of the Great Wall and the cities of the Khitai were captured by means of special tactics.

Jenghiz Khan and his heirs first entered into negotiations with the besieged. The latter thought that everything would be fine if they had a solemnly signed and sworn agreement in their hands—a piece of paper. They opened their gates and streamed out to the Mongol camp to negotiate with them. They hoped for a reduction in taxes, profitable trading and lasting peace. But then during the night the Mongols would force their way in through the unguarded gates, begin to plunder, murder and seize the easily-gotten spoils. A piece of paper was no hindrance to them at all. From other cities the Mongols demanded as sole tribute the handing-over of all swallows, doves and cats, which the townsmen willingly surrendered, glad to have escaped so lightly. But in the dim light of morning the besiegers released the birds and let the cats return home. Each creature bore on its tail a piece of glowing phosphorus. Mad with pain the creatures fled back to their nests and houses, with the result that the city went up in flames.

The Khan captured another town by damming a nearby river with the use of massive slave-labor. Then the Mongols pierced the dam and released the pent-up waters to wash away walls and fortifications.

A new and previous unknown type of conquest was threatening the cities of China. An order by Jenghiz Khan to his commanders read as follows: "I forbid kindness to be shown to the inhabitants of this land without my express command. It is not pity but severity which tames men's hearts. An enemy merely defeated is not tamed,

Polomie

Harvest scene in China, as seen by a European artist, Athanasius Kirchner, circa 1670.

Left: a Sung Emperor receives the representatives of a Taoist sect in his palace.
Right: Mongol horses grazing. China maintained close trade relations with Mongolia.

he will always hate his new master . . .

It is important that the Mongol armies should be preceded by a paralysing terror: that is more significant than that the foreign peoples should do our bidding willingly. Only fear and terror prepare the way of the conqueror. Therefore I order you: spread terror! Murder them all. . ."

In 1234 the kingdom of the Nüchen collapsed under the Mongol attacks, then in 1276–1279 followed the concentrated assault on the Sung state. That year, "the eighth of the sixty-fifth age of heaven, known as the Year of the Tiger", the ice of the imperial canal was late in breaking up. In Northern China the temperatures remained low until well into the Spring. When the waters of the melting snow had disappeared and the plains were dry once again, not a day passed without anxious news from the Great Wall. Ceaseless streams of refugees poured into the cities of Central China, bringing incredible reports about the size of the Mongol army.

The peasants hard-pressed by the tax-collector groaned: "Let them come! They can't take anything more from us!" And many of the merchants and citizens thought: "One can do business even with Mongols!" The last of the Sung emperors assembled a conscript army of peasants and citizens at the place in the Great Wall near where the enemy horsemen were massing. But Mangu Khan had no wish to attack there. With 150,000 horsemen and 300,000 remounts he crossed the desert of Tsachan and approached a particularly dilapidated section of the wall. The 150,000 men galloped through the moonless nights like a black stormcloud. With amazing speed they reached the spot where the Great Wall had been demolished by earth-

quakes and floodwaters. Almost without hindrance they broke through the wall and poured like a river into the provinces of Shansi and Shensi. A wave of fear went before the Mongols. Behind them they left only corpses and ruins. In the central provinces mothers sang this rhyme:

"The Tartars are here, the Tartars are there!
The Emperor has not anywhere!"

Once again the Chinese general Chu Sha Chu scraped together an army of 400,000 men and took up positions in the plain of Ta Tung Fu ready for the Mongol attack. But in the meantime Mangu Khan had brought in reserves of more than 300,000 fresh troops. The Sung army broke up, and the interior of China lay helpless before the Mongol hordes which now filled all its roads.

Mangu Khan and his brother and successor Kublai Khan (1260 onwards) were more intelligent and (thanks to their Uigur and Chinese tutors) more educated and humane than Jenghiz Khan had been. They understood that they could not dominate and hold on to the vast territories they had conquered simply by fear and terror. Thus a message of Mangu's announces:

"Tell them all that I have not come to chastise the poor and the peaceable but to punish the unjust and the guilty. In my dominions there shall be freedom of religion and respect for property and persons. Therefore open your gates and fortresses—I come in peace!"

Despite this the Sung put up a hard fight. But the people would not follow their rulers in a national war. The citizens heard with joy the news that their property would be respected, the

wretched, exploited peasants and workers heard wistfully of justice and greater freedom. The heroic general and stateman Wen T'ien Siang resisted in vain. In later days he was to be immortalised in plays, novels, verses and in the famous ivory carvings showing a general armed with a sword rescuing the last heir to the Sung dynasty, a child of three, from burning Nanking.

Province after province fell. Peking, captured in 1215, was renamed Tai Tu, in 1276 the Mongols captured Hangchow and Nanking and in 1277, after 17 years of fighting, at last took Canton. The Chinese fleet was defeated or destroyed, and in 1274 Kublai Khan ordered a new war fleet to sail to Japan. The Mongols spread over the entire face of South-East Asia. From Yunnan the tribes who wanted to remain free (the word is "Thai") fled over the mountains into what was to be Laos and Thailand, but in 1282 Kublai's horsemen reached Tongking and Annam. In 1287 Pagan, capital of

Illustrations of Marco Polo's voyage to China.
Left: scenes from a battle fought by the Khan against his enemies.
Right: Marco Polo at the court of Kublai Khan.

Burma, was plundered. All Indo-China came under Mongol rule, and in 1292 Mongol naval expeditions attacked Java.

The new master and Emperor of China, Kublai Khan (1271–1294), assumed the Chinese name Shi Tsu, called his dynasty that of the Yüan and took up residence in Peking ("Tai Tu"). For the first time in its history China had been conquered by foreigners.

5 China becomes Mongol and the Mongols Chinese...

Under Kublai Khan the Mongols completed the conquest and occupation of China. Their dominion over the "Middle Kingdom" reached its peak at this time. Incredible slaughter, destruction and suffering accompanied the birth of the Mongol empire. Chronicles and annals, especially numerous in the days of the Yüan, follow the mainstream of events. They describe the battles, taking of cities, the capture of the imperial family in Hangchow, the death of the last Emperor and the amazing expansion of the empire far beyond the former T'ang or Sung frontiers.

In narrating these events chroniclers also mention that from the days of Jenghiz Khan to the accession of Kublai Khan, a period of half a century of conquest, a certain change had come about among the leaders of the Mongols. The generation of Jenghiz Khan still belonged to the primitive barbaric and cruel horsemen of the steppes, a tribe risen from absolutely nothing, but the men who with Kublai Khan

took over power and government in China were members of a much younger generation who had had highly educated Uigur and Chinese tutors, teachers and advisers and were fascinated and captivated by the high culture of the conquered people. The Mongol horsemen did indeed conquer China's provinces, but Chinese culture conquered the hearts and minds of the Mongol leaders and in the course of time their troops as well.

Thus over the decades the Mongol conquest lost much of its terror, and instead of a primitive barbarian regime, a new dynasty took over, one which was Chinese in intent.

About the time when Kublai Khan finally assumed the title of emperor, the young Venetian Marco Polo (1254–1325) travelled with his father and uncle via Pamir to China, where he reached Kublai's court at Cambalu and later Tai Tu (Peking). As he was skilful at winning the friendship of the Mongol ruler, he rose to the position of Governor of Hangchow. Not until

seventeen years had passed did he return, a rich man, to Venice.

It was he who brought Europe the first accurate reports on China, the state of affairs existing there and the events which had taken place. But only a few believed Marco Polo. His native city gave him the mocking title "Messer Marco Millione".

How could anyone in Venice, the greatest city in Europe, boasting 1,400 bridges and 10,000 palaces, possibly believe that Hangchow had 14,000 bridges and about 80,000 palaces and that the yield of Hangchow's salt tax alone was greater than all the annual revenues of Venice?

Marco Polo reported that "Quinsay", as he called Hangchow, housed within its boundaries 1,600,000 families, about five million people. Despite these large numbers the strict order of an authoritarian state prevailed. Every head of a household was obliged, just as in the days of the Tsin, to fix a list to the door of his "kang" giving the name, sex, profession and status of

each resident. In inns, caravanserais and such places guests had to enter their names in a book which the police checked regularly. In this way officials and tax-collectors maintained a high level of supervision.

The city, a confusion of closely-packed buildings above which protruded the high faience roofs of temples, pagodas and palaces, covered an area of one hundred miles, branching out onto hills, into woods, bamboo groves, along waterways, coves, canals and lakes.

Four classes of persons lived in such cities, the Mongol overlords, the Se Mu (their ancillary peoples such as Tibetans, Tungus, Tangut, Turkomans and related tribes), then the Ch'in people of the northern provinces and last the Southern Chinese, who were the true Chinese people.

The administration of justice observed the same divisions amongst the people. The punishments meted out became harsher the further removed the criminal was from the ruling class. The grading of social ranks under Kublai Khan was as follows: 1. high officials of the court, 2. officials of the

provincial administrations, 3. lamas, 4. Taioist magicians, 5. doctors, 6. craftsmen and workers, 7. hunters, 8. traders and merchants, 9. scholars and followers of Confucius, 10. beggars. All Mongol warriors were assigned to the first two categories.

Concerning the administration and organisation of the state Marco Polo writes as follows:

"At the head of the administrative officials there is a civil and a military council, each consisting of twelve barons and responsible directly to the Emperor. The military council deals exclusively with military matters, especially the punishment, promotion and posting of officers and the disposition of troops. It has, however, only the right to put forward proposals —the final decision rests with the Emperor. In the supreme civil council twelve specially-appointed barons supervise the affairs of 34 provinces. The actual central administration is carried out by a judge and a staff of assistants and clerks . . .

It is the function of these judges in the central administration to choose provincial governors, who, on the re-

commendation of the supreme council, are appointed by the Emperor. The central administration in Tai Tu also deals with the collection of taxes and revenue, together with their administration and expenditure . . .

Then Marco Polo tells us of the paper money issued to cover the enormous costs of the constant military campaigns. Direct taxes were collected in accordance with lists, indirect taxes were levied on tea, iron, salt, spirits and silk. Horse-breeding and porcelain manufacture were state monopolies.

Marco Polo considered the taxation system a good one, were it not for the fact that of a population of about 50 to 60 million Chinese, the Mongol princes and the rich monasteries were exempt. The increasing issue of paper money caused inflation, so that in the end only 6 to 7 silver yen were being paid for a 10 yen note. That the vast apparatus of administration functioned at all in Yüan China the Venetian ascribed to two special circumstances. Firstly there were absolutely no childless families, so that there was always a surplus of labor, and secondly the people were incredibly moderate in their expectations. They lived almost exclusively on rice, buckwheat, millet and herbs, foods from plants which yielded a hundredfold.

"Of course the unfavorable weather sometimes causes crop failures. At such times Kublai Khan not only omits the usual tax, he sends specially-appointed officials amongst the people throughout the land to give them new seed corn. He is able to do this because in good years the government buys up great stocks of grain. In times of need this grain is sold at a quarter of its actual value. In a similar way the government helps when diseases break out

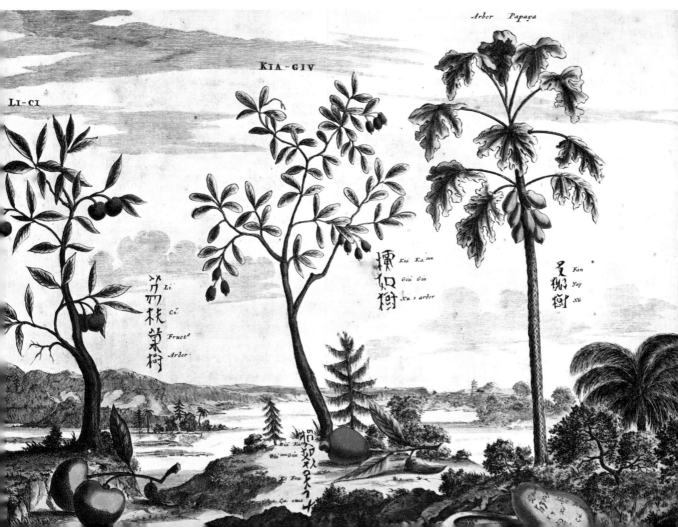

LI-CI

KIA-GIV

Arbor Papaya

amongst the livestock. Then the state farms provide breeding animals to build up the herds once again . . .''

Kublai Khan was very open to ideas of progress and especially to ideas from abroad. For this reason he was also interested in the Christian religion.

As early as 1245, during the Mongol invasion, Pope Innocent IV sent a delegation of missionaries to the Mongols. A companion of Saint Francis, Father Giovanni Plane de Carpini, and his fellow-friars got as far as Canton. He was astounded to see how many Frenchmen, Germans, Hungarians, Poles, Englishmen and Flemings he found among the yurts of the Mongols. All these were men who wanted to sell the achievements of Europe to the Mongol conquerors. For example, in the Altai Mountains there lived a whole colony of Thuringian miners digging for silver and gold. Carpini wrote his "Historia Mongolarum", which impressed King Louis XIV of France so much that he sent an embassy to Karakorum. The leader of the French embassy was the Flemish Franciscan Willem van Ruysbroek (1255). Kublai Khan even sent the Pope a message by the returning Marco Polo, asking him to send Christian missionaries. He was not averse to seeing China converted to Christianity, but unfortunately his message reached only a decaying papacy, which was shortly to go into exile at Avignon and had the Great Schism as well as other problems to deal with.

For all foreigners (as for the Mongol conquerors) one great hindrance in establishing closer contact with China was the difficulty of the Chinese language and script. Marco Polo himself, a very gifted linguist who on his eighteen-month journey to China learned perfectly Turkish, Arabic and Mongol, in all the 17 years of his residence in China never learned to speak or write Chinese properly. The same difficulties were experienced by Kublai Khan and his assistants. The mastery of the 70,000 characters which a scholar must know were an invincible obstacle to the deeper understanding of Chinese culture. That is why Kublai Khan attempted to introduce his "universal script" with the advice of the Tibetan Abbot Phagspa. The "Phagspa script", derided by the Chinese as "Mongol square script", is a combination of symbolic and phonetic script aiming at simplification. Nevertheless the Yüan period saw the appearance of many books with parallel texts, one in Mongol Square Script and the other in Persian-Cufic letters.

When the Mongol invasions began there were still decrees such as that of Mongko Khan's Prime Minister:

"The Chinese are useless for our purposes. Let them therefore be destroyed or driven away, so that the land they cultivate can serve as pasture for our horses!"

This extreme animosity between the races had cooled in the meantime. With every year spent by the Mongols in prosperity and ease in the midst of sophisticated Chinese culture, they developed more and more liking for the Chinese way of life. They began to learn rapidly, to adapt, to yield to the incredible absorbent power of China, but without the desire or the ability to lessen the distance between themselves, the conquering race, and the conquered. Many phases, of Mongol rule were characterised by tolerance.

The reign of Kublai Khan's successor saw a more peaceful situation: the Mongol conquest of the world came to a standstill. Internal unrest and financial difficulties forced the Yüan Emperors to give up any idea of capturing Burma or South Vietnam. The Mongol conquerors began to recognise the blessings of peace and the joys of good living and thus became militarily weakened. Emperor Jen Tsung (1311–1320) and his successors were weak rulers. The misrule of the Mongol ruling class, even of the Emperor in Peking, stank to high heaven: within three or four generations the conquerors had learned to enjoy their conquests and to yield to the culture of the conquered race.

The year 1354 was one in which harmony between heaven, earth and water was greatly impaired. First there was drought, then came typhoons and finally the rivers burst their banks. The masses of the people could clearly see that the "Son of Heaven", a dissolute man, was no longer living in accordance with divine harmony. As a result of famine the revolt of the "Red Kerchiefs" broke out. Additional provocation was given by new laws which bore harshly on the Chinese.

Once again it was a simple peasant "red faced as a pig, but of mighty strength of body", a Ming from the South called Chu Yüan-Chang, who placed himself at the head of the revolt. His mass armies, suddenly surging out of the immense countryside, fell upon the weakened, degenerate Mongols. In 1368 the "Ming peasants" stormed Peking. The last Mongol Emperor, Shun Ti, Kublai's great-grandson, with the Mongol name Timur, died in 1370 in the flight of his people back into the steppes of Central Asia. The interim period of the Yüan was at an end, and China was once again China, almost as if nothing terrible had occurred at all.

A Chinese chronicle writes of the last Yüan Emperor stories such as vic-

54

tors always write about the vanquished.

"Shun Ti was a superstitious, lustful, unprincipled weakling, who allowed himself to be too much influenced by low-ranking lamas. He attempted to become a mandarin and only strayed into all kinds of magic and mystical practices, which he only half understood and which strengthened his tendency to immorality."

Merely playing with a sophisticated culture, the grandsons of once warlike and naively self-confident conquerors lost an empire which they had become too weak to retain and which they were incapable of shaping and governing. These "half Chinese" now streamed back to their steppes. In the traditional

way a Chinese poet painted a watercolor and wrote these verses with it:

"Five weeping willows are mirrored
  in the water;
a cherry-tree fills my window.
The mountain moon hangs in the
  creepers, shining as if polished.
I sing to the zither: the wind sighs
  in the pine-trees . . ."

(Ni-Tsan, 1370)

The victor Chu Yüan-chang chose as his seat of government a great city on the Yangtze, Nanking, for he was a "Ming", a Southern Chinese. As the new Emperor of a native Chinese dynasty he took the name Hung-wu of the "Ming" dynasty.

"Ming" means literally "brilliance". The new dynasty was to decide the fate of China from 1368 to 1644.

Though the Mongol invasion must have seemed a catastrophe to those who experienced it, later generations considered that the hundred years or so of foreign, often hostile, domination had produced great cultural achievements. It was one of the benefits of Mongol rule that the great road from China through Persia and Russia, provided with posting stations and securely policed, now fostered more rapid communications between East and West and thus opened the door to foreign cultural influences. Under the Yüan emperors this brought about that significant tolerance in religious matters which gave Islam and Christianity, as well as Buddhism and Taoism, full scope. In 1287 the Tripitaka, a collection of Buddhist writings, was reprinted on wooden tablets. In 1307 Johan de Monte Corvino was Archbishop of Peking, Hangchow also became the site of a cathedral and the Muslim Sayid Edjell made Yunnan a center of Mohammedan cultural life.

Under the Mongols the language of scholars had developed into the general standard language of all Chinese. Novels, ballads and most of all the drama flourished in a way in keeping with the agitated character of the times. More than 80 poets of classical reputation produced plays and novels — tales of Mongol adventures, tales of robbers, stories of Chinese resistance and heroism.

Even science had its triumphs. The mathematician Kiu Shao wrote a book about determinate and indeterminate equations, the Persian Jamal ud Din (Cha Ma Lu Ting) devised an astronomical calendar. In the great cities observatories were built whose precision instruments were similar to those of medieval Europe.

At the siege of the fortress of Siang Yang, circa 1271, a chronicle mentions for the first time the use of cannons, shells and gunpowder, an invention which appeared in Europe a few decades later. Its route passed through Persia, Arabia, North Africa, Moorish Spain and thence to the Rhine.

The geographer Chu Sse-pen drew and printed the first world atlas about the year 1300.

Influenced by the Mongols, who as a nomadic people felt a close affinity with the landscape and animals, particularly horses, painting produced a new style, that of soft-toned landscapes and picturesque representations of riders, horses and exciting battle-scenes. But Chinese painters also discovered the small and unpretentious things of life—insects, flowers, butterflies and fishes. The arabesques of the Middle East, the ornamentation of the Persians, the age-old patterns of the Scythians now appeared on porcelain, in the newly-developed art of carpet-making, in the adornment of bronzes and on carved stonework. The porcelain glazers' favorite colors were a delicate white and cobalt blue.

The Mongol period had not merely interrupted China's cultural development, it had indeed fertilised it anew and prepared the ground for the great Ming period (1368–1644), a totally Chinese cultural Golden Age.

The Temple of Heaven in Peking, built under the Ming in 1420.

6 Ming - the Great Brilliance

As so often in Chinese history, it was a popular movement of the oppressed peasantry, led by a scion of the common people, which toppled a disordered government. For the third time since the Han a simple peasant ascended the Dragon Throne and founded a new harmonious dynasty.

The revolt which had defeated the corrupt and debilitated Mongols had, as well as nationalist, distinctly social motives, and the rebellious masses demanded the redistribution of property and the reform of taxation in accordance with equality and justice.

For at the end of the period of Mongol domination the peasant population, being the most defenseless section of the people, had been bedevilled by demands for taxes and forced labor on roads, canals and river embankments, whilst more than a million conquerors were free of all taxation and burdens and the gentry in the cities used bribery and corruption to come to a satisfactory arrangement with Mongol officials.

This privileged class of rich merchants, great landowners (who lived in palaces in the cities and through their stewards extorted vast sums from small tenant farmers), moneylenders and grasping usurers, the traditional nobility and members of rich and ancient families, had been far from delighted at the outbreak of a national uprising. In fact they even raised auxiliary troops for their Mongol overlords, because they were afraid that the insurgents would deprive them of their property. By contrast, the corruption of the Mongols suited them very well.

Apart from these important sections of the population, the masses and the privileged gentry, there had grown

up a petty bourgeoisie of the cities, consisting of scholars, literati, artists, tradesmen, craftsmen and small businessmen. This class supported the rebellious peasantry for social reasons, and it was amongst its members that first began that pure Chinese nationalism which in the end swept the peasant leader Chu Yüan-chang into Nanking, Peking and the Throne of Heaven.

The development of a middle class at the beginning of the Ming period is one of the characteristics of the new age in Chinese history.

It was only too natural that after more than a hundred years of foreign oppression and having to endure an alien dynasty the reaction of the Chinese should be feelings of nationalism. From the very beginning the China of the Ming period showed itself distrustful of everything foreign and hostile towards foreigners. The doors to the outside world kept open by the Yüan emperors were closed again, the trade routes fell into disuse, seafaring was neglected and contact with other nations resulted in feelings of distrust.

For that reason the most important achievement and most conspicuous legacy of the Ming was the total seclusion of China, especially from Central Asia, from whose vast spaces disaster had come in the past. The Ming Emperors had the "Great Wall" of Shu Huang Ti (221–210 B.C.) replaced by a fortified wall of solid masonry.

Parallel to such defensive measures all foreign elements in politics, economic and cultural life introduced in the Mongol period were eradicated, the language purged of mongolisms, the racial laws diffaming the native Chinese abolished and all foreigners dismissed from offices of state.

As the Mongols had been very tolerant in religious matters, while favoring the Taoism more congenial to them, now under the Ming there was a

明福建布政參議陳公如綸

詠三懷詩
却百金贈
義道眧憲
氣導武宗

less tolerant tendency, which led to the oppression of Taoists and shamans, magicians and Tibetan forms of religion and favored the Neo-Confucianism of the school of Chu Hsi. Gradually the followers of Master Kung, with their own ethic and concept of the State, took over the conduct of affairs in the Ming empire.

Chu Yüan-chang called the first Ming Emperor T'ai Tsu but known to History as Hung-wu (1368–1398), was a typical peasant who had risen in the world from modest beginnings. He trusted in his physical strength, his family and his old village friends. As he was unceasingly suspicious of the coterie of learned scholars and the mandarins left over from the Mongol period and never rid himself of the complexes of the ill-educated, whenever he had grounds for suspicion, in times of crisis and personal tensions he had thousands of people, courtiers, officials or provincials, executed, indeed in the early years he was not afraid to carry out such executions in person. He drew his provincial governors from the new imperial house and from amongst his village friends, thus creating dangers for future governments.

A true peasant, his very first measures were directed to the reorganisation of agriculture, which was in complete disorder. Depopulated areas

were settled once again, new surveys distributed the land according to fairer principles, a kind of "agrarian reform" was his gift to the peasant masses who had given him their support. Then Emperor T'ai Tsu carried out a reform of the currency, paper money became the main means of payment, and a tax reform shared the burdens in a more just manner. The preparation of a new, epoch-making code of laws, the "Ta Ming-lü" was entirely due to his initiative.

His government was headed by a Chancellor who supervised the six main ministries. In such a way order returned to large parts of the empire. But at his own court T'ai Tsu allowed eunuchs to take up important posts, tolerated favorites, authoritarian officials and generals who meddled in politics. This atmosphere of intrigue and arrogance produced the first storm-clouds immediately after T'ai Tsu's death.

Displacing T'ai Tsu's nominated successor, a prince entered into a conspiracy with eunuchs and other courtiers which enabled him to ascend the Dragon Throne. It was the fourth son of a minor wife, Prince Chu Ti of Yen, who snatched the crown of the Ming. As Emperor Ch'eng Tsu (1403–1424) he became indisputably one of the most important rulers of the Ming dynasty.

But first he had to wage a five-year war of succession which laid waste great areas of China. Even the Mongols attacked again, though their efforts met with no success. Japanese pirates seized the opportunity and plundered the coasts.

Because of the insecurity of sea travel, the Grand Canal between the lower reaches of the Yangtze and Peking was widened so that it could be used by quite large ships.

After the end of the civil war Emperor Ch'ang Tsu attempted to regain control of the sea by building a gigantic fleet. Under the leadership of the Mohammedan eunuch Cheng Ho seven expeditions were made, to the Malay Archipelago, Ceylon, India, the Persian Gulf and East Africa. One of these took 63 large junks with a complement of 25,000 men to the coasts of Arabia and Africa. This made such a great impression on the rest of the world that 16 states sent tribute to the Ming Emperor. Under Ch'eng Tsu the Mongols were again, this time decisively, beaten at the River Onon. He was, however, unable to prevent the loss of the province of North Vietnam in 1431.

But even under Emperor Ying Tsung (1436–1449) signs of decay became visible in the Ming dynasty. The Thai, Laotian, Miao and Viet tribes, driven out of South China, particularly Yunnan, and into Indo-China by the Mongols and Chinese, were finally subdued to some extent after much warfare, but the area remained a trouble-spot for the next five hundred years. In the meantime the civil service of the Ming empire expanded greatly: 100,000 civil servants and 80,000 officers dominated every aspect of the nation's life. The imperial court in Peking became a hotbed of intrigue.

Under Emperor Shi Tsung (1522–1566) the once mighty imperial fleet had declined to such an extent that Japanese pirates not only plundered the coasts but sailed up the Yangtze, landed in Nanking and besieged the second city of the empire. Unrest grew in the northern provinces.

One of the most energetic Ming rulers was Shen Tsung (1573–1619). During the campaign of the Japanese condottiere Hideyoshi (1592–1598) he came to the aid of the hard-pressed Koreans, but was beaten back: In 1604 China had once again to pay tribute to the Mongol Jahar tribes to maintain peace.

As Emperor Shen Tsung had no issue by his principal wife, he tried to make the son of a concubine his successor. But the party of the eunuchs, generals and mandarins started the "Conspiracy of the Tung Lin Library"

in favor of another prince. After the Emperor's death the court was dominated by intrigues and palace revolts. Despite the large numbers of officials the tax system had fallen into confusion. Famine, successive drought and flood, oppression of the peasantry and tenant farmers and the insecurity of the imperial frontiers once again brought the state to the brink of chaos, so that in 1622 the sect of the "White Lotus" rose in rebellion. Gang-leaders took control of distant provinces, peasant armies marched on Peking, so that in 1644 the Ming general Wu San-kwei could think of no better recourse than to call on the Manchus of the North for aid.

Thus came the downfall of the Ming, and the Manchus entered the stage of history.

When years ago the Mongols had been ejected from China, peoples of mainly Tungus origin had settled in Western Manchuria. In 1583 Nurhachu, chieftain of the Gioro Tungus, carved the Manchurian Empire out of the conquered provinces of Northern China. The same pattern of events took place as always when Central Asia suddenly seized power: a strong man knitted together previously disunited peoples into a highly-organised military force. Nurhachu's most brilliant idea was to divide the Tungus into four, later eight, "banners" or army corps, which had a separate independent existence but acted in concert with the others. First he took the title of "Khan", then in 1616 that of Emperor. The "Kin Empire" of the Manchu, with Mukden as capital, stretched from the Amur to Korea and the Sea of Japan. In 1629, when Ming China was torn by inner conflict and the revolt of the "White Lotus" was bringing its peasant armies northwards, the Manchu "banners" sud-

denly broke through the Great Wall and surrounded the Ming capital, Peking, in a wide semicircle.

A chronicle describes thus the end of the Ming period: "People were reduced to eat the bark from the trees and the roots of the grass, and when this was not enough, they ate soil. But the Ming emperors nevertheless extorted higher and higher taxes to finance their military operations against rebels and the Manchus."

In this troubled period the Jesuit Father Schall was director of the imperial observatory in Peking. Now he was relieved of his duties as astronomer and appointed one of the directors of the imperial cannon foundries. The Jesuits produced the bronze cannon with which the Ming defended themselves against attack.

Because of the famine many peasants had turned to banditry. The rebel army of Li Tsu swelled into a flood and surged along the valleys of the Hoang Ho and Yangtze Kiang, murdering all those who owned any kind of property.

Chaos spread with lightning speed. The last Ming army, led by general Wu San-kuei, was defending the Great Wall to the North of Peking, but the rebels were approaching from the South. The vast city of Peking was in an uproar, the inhabitants of its slums rose in rebellion and swarmed into the Imperial City. Screaming mobs advanced on the "pink walls" of the Sin Ching Palace. Messengers hurried to the Great Wall to recall the army of General Wu San-kuei.

It was too late. The rebels were already storming the palace.

It was then that the Ming Emperor gave up the fight and left the palace. In the park was an artificial hill, called the "Shining Hill" (and in the nineteenth century the "Hill of Coals"). The Em-

Chinese New Year Festival with lanterns, one of which is in the shape of a carp, meaning good luck.

peror Szu Tsung ascended the hill and looked long over the rooftops of his burning capital. The cannons thundered ceaselessly from the beleaguered walls, the cries of battle could be heard from afar and flocks of ravens approached over the wide plains of clay. They sensed that a banquet awaited them.

Then Emperor Szu Tsung looped a purple cord over the branch of a pine-tree and hanged himself on the summit of the "Shining Hill".

On the very same day the rebels stormed the "Forbidden City", sacked the palaces and found the corpse of the "Son of Heaven". In the sash of his yellow silken robe was fastened a petition addressed to the rebel leader and asking, even in such extreme circumstances, for mercy for his people.

At the same time General Wu San-kuei, now firmly in league with the Manchus, was advancing on Peking at the head of his army, closely followed by the "banners" of the Manchus. Disaster was approaching, not through the rebels but again through foreigners, this time the armies of the Manchus.

The nationalist Ming Empire had always been distrustful, indeed hostile, towards foreigners. But fate decreed that the Ming should constantly be in contact with them.

Since the Age of Discovery and the European Renaissance the world had become larger in one sense but in an-other its parts had moved closer to each other. America had emerged from the darkness of history, Spanish, Portuguese, soon English, French and Dutch ships sailed the oceans of the world, seeking the treasures of the earth or bringing Christian missionaries. In 1511 the Portuguese established themselves in Malaya, in 1517 Portuguese ships landed at Canton, in 1545 foreigners obtained, with great difficulty, permission to settle at the port of Ningpo.

When the Portuguese joined the Japanese in coastal piracy, they were expelled. In 1557 they occupied the trading post of Macao. At this time (circa 1552) the Apostle of Japan, St. Francis Xavier, died on the island of

64

Sancian off the coast of Macao. He had not received permission to enter Ming China.

The years 1579–1598 saw the swift Russian advance into the vast emptiness of Siberia, where they quickly set up an enormous colonial empire. In 1643, only a year before the end of the Ming dynasty, their Cossack troops reached the Amur, where they set up walled forts.

In 1564–1565 the Spaniards landed on the islands which they called the Philippines after their king. They too were interested in trade with China and set up trading posts in Canton in 1604 and 1607.

Dutch merchants established themselves on the Chinese island of Formosa (1622), and the English made their appearance in Amoy and Canton in 1637.

China was like an old lion surrounded by a circle of waiting hyenas and jackals. His teeth had become weak and rotten, but he was still a lion of enormous strength. By a policy of deliberately excluding the outside world China had kept itself apart from the rising tide of developments in Europe, the dawn of a rationalist, technological age fascinated by the sciences. What surprised the traditional wisdom of the Chinese and excited their admiration, was the Europeans' vast knowledge of astronomy, physics, mathematics, chemistry and mechanics.

That fact was realised by the Jesuit Matteo Ricci (1552–1610), who following in the footsteps of St. Francis Xavier, sought entry into Ming China. Through his excellent command of languages, his wide knowledge of modern European technology and physics he won the friendship of great mandarins. He was first allowed to live in Canton, then to move to Peking on the recommendation of Chinese friends. There he won over the Emperor, an enthusiastic collector of clocks, by presenting him with a fine timepiece. As astronomer, architect and mechanical engineer he attained the rank of "po hi". The Chinese called him "Doctor Li" and soon accepted his religious doctrine as well. The Jes-

The Chinese counterpart of the fertility goddess Cybele.

uits, then other Catholic orders were granted permission to enter China.

Thus it was mainly Jesuits who took charge of the regulation of the calendar, observatories and cannon foundries in the Emperor's service. They laid out parks in the formal French style, built fountains like those at Versailles, taught painters and bronze-founders to work in the European Baroque style and wrote many books on Chinese culture and customs. This relationship soon had its effect on Europe: chinoiseries became the height of fashion at the courts of Europe's absolute rulers. There, pagodas and Ming temples were built, Chinese silk was used for clothes and soon (1720) porcelain was invented. Chinoiseries such as lacquer chests, cloisonné dishes and vases, porcelain in all shapes and colors, made in Europe's rapidly-expanding porcelain factories, enriched the cultural life of Europe. Even the grasping traders, business-men, captains and colonial rulers of the period, who were dividing up the world from India to Africa and the Americas by means of force, deceit, cannons and diplomacy, and swarmed over these exotic lands like parasites, seizing their treasures and raw materials, were forced to realise that China was an ancient, powerful and highly-developed culture. They therefore penetrated the Chinese Empire with a certain amount of caution by following the routes taken by the missionaries.

The culture of the Ming was worthy of admiration. In many fields it was even superior to that of Europe, it was only its technical and scientific development which had not kept pace. Europeans were amazed by the works of Chinese architecture, by the Great Wall, whose vast battlements, dotted with square towers and fortresses wound for 2,500 miles over mountain peaks; by the mighty palaces of Nanking, Canton or Peking; they saw the pagodas and temples, the famous "Altar of Heaven" and the "Temple of Heaven" in the "Forbidden City". Chinese painting, with its delicate feminine portraits, "bamboo paintings" of exquisite harmony and form, wonderfully harmonious watercolors of landscapes, flowers, people and animals, meant for Europeans the discovery of a strange new style and expressive power which Europe's Baroque and Mannerist art could not match.

The ceramics, with their three-color glazes (mainly Ming Blue, and Ming Pink on brilliant Porcelain White) were delightful. Everything made by Chinese artists and craftsmen in the way of inlaid or finely-carved ivory, sandalwood carving, cast bronzes, cloisonné, painted screens, engraved tea-kettles, gods and heroes in metal or stone, splendid lacquer-work and carpets from Chinese Turkestan, were valuable commodities for European markets. But connoisseurs of China, mainly Jesuits, also praised the flourishing novel of the Ming, its splendid plays, the Peking operas and the rich diversity of music. Dramatic poetry reached new heights in the Ming period.

Apart from this traditional scholarship was fostered: in the Han-Lin Academy in Peking, for example, more than 200 scholars wrote the gigantic "Yung Lo Ta Tien" encyclopedia which was compiled in 22,937 books, some 200 years before the first European encyclopedia appeared.

Other works produced about this time included catalogues, dictionaries, and an impressive array of books on morality, mathematics, astronomy, geography and medicine.

Intellectual life flourished in the field of religion as well. Neo-Confucianism and Buddhism developed a rich literature. In the Ming period, Abbot Tsung K'apa (1357–1419) reformed the lamas and founded the order of "Yellow Lamas", whose saffron robes the Europeans now saw as often as the traditional robes of the "Red Lamas".

This then was the "Middle Kingdom" which now lost its native dynasty in the invasion from the North, collapsed and became the target of European imperialists and colonialists.

Once again a new epoch in Chinese history was beginning.

The Emperor Shi Tsung, on a tour of inspection in his southern provinces, receives the homage of his subjects.

7 The Manchus - Between Past and Present

Too late to help the Ming Emperor, the relieving force of General Wu San-kuei advanced towards Peking. When it came within sight of the walls, the rebel leader Li Tzu collected together the loot he and his rebels had taken from the palaces of the capital, had everything loaded onto hundreds of carts and fled southwards. The "White Lotus" gangs were pursued by the regular troops as far as the Hwang-Ho.

But Genral Wu San-kuei himself was closely followed by the Manchu banners. The Khan of the Manchus, Fu-lin, was proclaimed Emperor at Peking (contrary to the Manchu agreement with Wu San-kuei) took the name Shih Tsu (1644–1662) and called his new dynasty "Ch'ing"—the Chinese normally use the term "Manchu" only as a term of contempt.

The mass of the Chinese population let the conquerors have their own way. Things could hardly have become worse for them under the Manchus than under the later Ming dynasty. Three hundred years before there had been another period of foreign domination, the Yüan period, which lasted only a century. Nobody guessed that this period of foreign domination would last more than 250 years (1644–1912).

An external circumstance soon inflamed people's emotions. The Tungus Manchus, though taller and more strongly-built than the Chinese, were nevertheless physically very similar to them. They had high cheekbones, yellow skin and slanting eyes like the Mongols. But the way in which they wore their jetblack hair was different. Whilst the Chinese either let their hair grow long, bound in a knot at the back of the head, or cut it to a medium length, the Manchu conquerors shaved their hair from forehead to crown and plaited the strands of hair on the back of the head into a characteristic pigtail.

Sheng Tsu, an Emperor of the Manchu dynasty, depicted by A. Kirchner.

By this pigtail a Manchu could be distinguished from a Chinese even at a distance. The conquerors now wanted the subjugated "Ming Chinese" to declare their friendship and loyalty by adopting the same hairstyle. In the course of the conquest of China the Emperor Shih Tsung decreed that all those who acknowledged the Manchu dynasty should wear a pigtail.

In the meantime the Ming Prince Fu based himself at Nanking, where General Wu San-kuei joined forces with him. After the Manchus had reorganised their "banners" and by hypocritical negotiations and cunning propaganda had managed to procure a period of peace in which to rest, reorganise and pacify the northern provinces, they struck once again. Their battlecry was: "The pigtail or death!"

Dreadful atrocities were committed. In the pursuit of the fleeing Prince Fu the Manchu troops advanced on the strongly-defended city of Chia-ting in South China and set it ablaze with cannon-fire. Its citizens and the Ming garrison surrendered. On entering the city the Manchu general gave orders that only those wearing the pigtail were to be left alive. But as pigtails do not grow overnight and the "ko hat" had not yet been invented, 78,000 people were slaughtered by the conquerors.

The Manchus pressed on irresistibly. In 1645 they took Nanking, in 1650 Canton, the Ming family fell into the hands of the conquerors, the outer provinces as far as Annam and Burma fell and by 1659 the Manchus had succeeded in bringing the vast empire and all its dependencies completely under control.

Then, in South China, the "ko hat" was invented; a straw hat with a pigtail fixed to it. People wore it in the street,

Horsemen from the Mongolian plains, in those days the terror of almost the whole European and Oriental world.

and at home in the kang one could be a Ming Chinese again.

Only on the seas was the old régime able to put up a fierce fight. General Wu San-kuei put the rest of his Ming army on board a fleet of junks. Together with the half-Japanese Koxinga he became a much-feared pirate who even sailed up the rivers of China and plundered cities. For a time the Manchus had to evacuate a strip 12 to 15 miles wide along the China and Yellow Seas, for the pirates had total control of the islands, bays and searoutes.

Despite this resistance the Manchu Emperors had the land in a firm grip and established their rule more firmly by reorganising the shattered state. On the Ming pattern they organised affairs under six ministries (pu): Li (Ministry of the Interior), Hu (Finance), Li (a different character, Culture and Education), Ping (War), Sing (Justice) and Kung (Construction). Soon they added a Ministry for the Colonies, which included Mongolia, East Turkestan, Tibet and Burma.

Like the Mongols they passed racial laws which contained a ban on marriages between Ming Chinese and Manchus, made the wearing of the pigtail obligatory and for a time forbade the unpleasant Chinese custom of binding women's feet.

A period of peace lasting 150 years brought relative prosperity to the country, especially a flowering of world trade in silk, porcelain, tea and later opium. A class of big businessmen and bankers arose, the so-called "hong merchants" who monopolised the financing and development of markets.

The Emperor Sheng Tsu (1662–1722) was the most important member of the whole dynasty. He became a great patron of the arts and sciences, and brought the economy to a

very high level of prosperity. In 1683 he laid siege to the island of Formosa, previously a stronghold of pirates and the Dutch, and the first place in China to grow the opium poppy. When in 1685–1687 there was a clash with the advancing Russians on the Amur, the Emperor negotiated the peace of Nerchinsk, by which China regained all territories occupied by the Russians and was allowed to set up military posts along the "Black Dragon" (Amur). Far to the South, in the high country of Tibet, the Manchus built forts and set up garrisons. Lhasa, the holy city of the Dalai Lama, even became the residence of the Chinese military governor. Although the Emperor Sheng Tsu ruled a vast, united and pacified empire, he was under pressure from foreigners who wanted to break

into the gigantic Chinese market. In 1715 the first British "factory" was set up in Canton. In 1722 he was forced to grant the Russians permission to open a trading post in Peking and in 1727 the trade pact of Kiachta was signed with the Russians.

This pact took place in the reign of the Emperor Shih Tsung (1723 to 1735), who under aggressive foreign pressure ordered a total ban on all Christian missionary activity and the persecution of all Christians. The ruling Confucians labelled the Christians "enemies of the state" and harbingers of foreign invasion. But the Russians, threatening from the North, were actually allowed to set up a permanent Christian mission in Peking. The danger from outside and thus the feeling of xenophobia became even more pro-

nounced under the Emperor Kao Tsung (1736–1795). In 1757 all Chinese ports were closed to European merchants, and all the pleas of English, Dutch and French ships' captains were in vain. Only Canton, where foreign trade was in the hands of the merchants of the Hong, was allowed to remain a trading port for foreign merchants.

In 1751, under the Emperor Kao Tsung, Tibet finally became a Chinese protectorate. A Chinese military expedition went to Burma in 1765 to 1769, and another great military achievement was the penetration in 1791/92 of the Gurkha regions of Nepal and Sikkim, which acknowleged Chinese suzerainty. Chinese troops also fought in Kansu, against Mohammedan rebels, against the ever-

Left: a Manchu Emperor travels through his provinces.
This page, top: The Emperor enters a small Chinese town.
Bottom: Mongolian deer hunt organised for the Emperor.
A painting in the Chinese manner by Father Castiglioni.

unruly Mongols, Formosan rebels and the "White Lotus" gangs in Shantung.

Despite these visible signs of the Manchu Empire's military and political energy, unrest was clearly growing in China. Constant rebellions, like that of the "Heavenly Reason" sect of 1813 which led to battles around the Imperial Palace in Peking or that of the "White Lotus", which led to the impoverishment of the provinces of Hupei, Shensi and Szechwan, indicated lasting discontent with a dynasty which remained in spirit foreign to the Chinese and allowed the flood-protection embankments to fall into decay, allowed bankers and great landowners to take more and more control of the nation's wealth, whilst the condition of the peasant farmers

and small tradesmen got worse and worse. From abroad there was growing pressure from foreigners, whose heavily-armed warships cruised around China's coasts and controlled the sea routes. In the reign of the Emperor Jen Tsung (1796–1820) Lord Amherst came to Peking to negotiate a commercial treaty. As he refused to perform the "kotow"—prostration before the emperor—the talks were broken off. Europeans were, as before, subject to Chinese jurisdiction (1816).

In the meantime the British, represented by the East India Company, were doing a roaring trade in opium. The opium grown in British-controlled Bengal was transported by the shipload to the British trading-station at Wei-ha Wei near Canton and, despite the imperial ban, was imported into China at a profit of 1,000%, the "merchants of the Hong" (rich merchants and bankers) participating in the venture. In 1834 the East India Company's monopoly was abolished, but the opium trade continued with the approval of the British government. In 1839 the Imperial Commissionar Liu-Tse-hsü had 20,000 cases of opium confiscated and expelled the British drug importers. Several Hong bankers, including one of Lin's brothers, were beheaded.

England's most sacred things were here being attacked—money and trade. In 1840 the Royal Navy, which ruled the waves, sent vessels under Captain Elliot to seize Hong Kong, proclaiming it part of the British Empire. British ships captured Amoy, Ningpo, Shanghai and Chinkiang. Warships destroyed the Tiger Forts on the Pearl River, bombarded Canton and set it on fire. A unit of the Royal Navy even sailed up the Yangtze-Kiang and opened fire on the vener-

able city of Nanking, destroying the world-famous "Porcelain Pagoda".

Abruptly China was forced to realise its technical inferiority and its deficiencies in military, and especially naval, matters. It was defenseless against the dwarf from the West which attacked with iron-built steamships and long-range artillery. So it was that the Manchu emperor under the Treaty of Nanking in 1842 ceded Hong Kong (and soon afterwards Kowloon opposite it) to Great Britain, had to open the ports of Canton, Amoy, Ningpo, Foochow and Shanghai to European trade, sanction the opium trade and grant the foreigners consular rights and their own legal jurisdiction. As a penalty China had to pay reparations of 21 million U.S. dollars. There fol-

lowed treaties with France and the United States. The foreigners had burst through the gates of the empire.

The humiliating defeat of the Manchus stirred the national pride of the Ming Chinese. Social stress, corruption amongst officials and Hong merchants, financial exploitation by landowners and bankers had long been building up an ominous tension amongst the peasantry. Once again the scales tipped in favor of chaos.

The answer of the Chinese masses was the Taiping Rebellion of 1850. A teacher named Hung Hsiu-ch'uan, influenced by Christian and Socialist ideas, proclaimed the rebellion. At first only his relatives, 20,000 cousins, came to his aid, but later hundreds of thousands of peasants and coolies

joined the rebellion. Under the Emperor Wen Tsun (1851–1861) the Taiping Rebellion became Manchu China's gravest problem. When in 1854 the foreigners took over the supervision of the Chinese customs, the uprising, fanned by nationalist feelings, spread even further and before long covered most of the provinces.

In the end the Manchus had to accept British help in order to retain their power at all. Major Gordon (later in Khartoum to be the victim of the Mahdi's rebellion) led foreign auxiliaries. In 1856–57 Great Britain officially intervened in this confusion with troops and ships in the so-called "Lorcha War". A Franco-British expedition captured and plundered Canton in 1857. The weakness of China

Tartars bringing the
Manchu Emperor tribute in the
form of horses.
Left: The great Lama Temple
in Peking, built about 1750.

77

From top: French cartoon on the British opium trade, about 1840. The port of Canton with British mission and warehouse building, about 1849. The port of Macao about 1850.

was turned to account by the Russians, who forced the recognition of the Amur Province as Russian territory by the treaty of Aigun in 1858.

In 1860, after a Franco-British fleet had bombarded the Taku forts, an ex-peditionary corps landed and seized Peking. The European Christians sacked the magnificent Summer Palace outside the city. The exhibits of the Asian sections of many a European museum were bought for a song in

Scenes from the Taiping Rebellion.

those days, and many Chinese art treasures came to adorn English country houses and French châteaux.

Once again the Russians profited from China's misery by annexing the coastal province East of the Ussuri and forcing China to agree to their making Vladivostok a Russian port.

Massive foreign intervention finally put down the Taiping Rebellion in 1862–1864. This attempt to bring about a social and national liberation of the Chinese people was drowned in blood.

In the Far East the militarily superior foreigners helped themselves to anything they fancied: in 1859 the French occupied Saigon and later all

Scenes from the Chino-Japanese War of 1894–95. The superiority of the Japanese was quite obvious.

Tongking and Annam (North Vietnam) and in 1863 Cambodia. Japan, beginning its Meiji period of assimilation of European civilisation, took over the "protection" of Korea (1876) and began to build up a colony there. By threats of war Great Britain gained new bases and commercial advantages. In 1886 China had to cede Burma to Great Britain, and the Russians extended their Siberian empire to Liaotung, Port Arthur and Dairen. In the Chino-Japanese War of 1894–95 the badly-equipped Manchu army was defeated by the "island dwarfs", and by the Treaty of Shimonoseki (1895) was forced to cede Korea, Formosa and the Pescadores to Japan. In 1896—1900 the Europeans exacted further concessions, and in 1897 that laggard in the race for national unity and Imperialist expansion, the German Empire, made Kiaochow a naval base. China agreed to a Shantung Railroad and to foreign management of the Shantung Coalfield.

The reign of the Emperor Te Tsung (1875—1908), in whose stead first the Manchu Prince Kung and later the tough, clever Dowager Empress Tzu-Hsi ruled, became a spectacle of total national enfeeblement. Eunuchs and fossilised Mandarins controlled Peking and political decisions were increasingly restricted to the imperial palace in Peking. Accordingly it is little wonder that the spirit of the Chinese people, as it always did in times of decline and chaos, rose up in rebellion against a dynasty, moreover a foreign one, which could no longer maintain the ancient harmony of forces, let alone give the country back its self-respect and usher it into the modern age.

In 1900—1905 widespread uprisings took place. The "White Lotus" reappeared. A sect called the "Great Knife" or "Boxers" preached hatred of the foreigners and in 1900 launched a furious attack on them, tolerated by the Manchu régime.

Left, from top: cartoons from the great age of European and Japanese colonialism and imperialism in China which brought about the country's fragmentation and decline.

A joint intervention by the European powers resulted from the murder of the German Ambassador, von Ketteler. It was led by the German general von Waldersee. The Taku forts, Tientsin and finally Peking were all taken and foreign troops marched into the Imperial Palace.

The peace treaty, signed by twelve

countries, obliged China to pay an indemnity of 450 million taels and provided for a foreign military presence in foreign legations, the guarding of the Shantung Railroad and the fortification of the legation quarter of Peking by foreign troops.

But China had still not reached the nadir of its shame and helplessness. In 1904–05 the Russo-Japanese War was in full swing. After the Japanese victory China had to agree to their taking over Russian rights on the Liaotung peninsula. In 1910 Russia and Japan came to terms over Manchuria, while ignoring Chinese rights in this, the home province of the Tsin dynasty. In the same year Korea was annexed by Japan.

China was an open market for European, Japanese and American trade. All business transactions were conducted according to the rules of the more powerful foreigners. Special legal provisions were made for the latter, who could only be brought to book by their own legations. The Americans, French and English transported ship-

loads of cheap Chinese coolies to their plantations and colonial mines, to work in conditions of slavery. Then, in 1905, the USA forbade Chinese immigration into the "Land of the Free".

The situation had reached the stage where a spark would suffice to set off national and social revolution. The minds of educated Chinese were already influenced by ideas of Socialism, democracy and modern science brought from the West.

In 1905 Minister Tuan Fang promised political reform and a constitution. The youth of China passionately demanded sweeping reforms on the European pattern and a reconstruction of Chinese power to a level befitting a great nation.

But the Empress Dowager Tzu Hsi stubbornly closed her ears to all this. When students and professors handed over to her the funds collected from the Chinese people for the construction of a modern navy, she philosophised on the pointlessness of all weapons of war and asked: "But where are the great fleets of history? They are all at the bottom of the sea . . . But I intend to build an unsinkable ship which will bring joy to future generations . . ."

She then gave orders for a tea pavilion in the shape of a ship to be built in the lake of the Summer Palace.

On the death of the progressive-minded minister all reforms seemed endangered (1909). The last Empress, Tzu Hsi, followed him to the grave and with her the last Manchu resistance collapsed for the new ruler, the Hsüan T'ung Emperor, was only two years old. Change and revolution were imminent.

Once again a period of Chinese history was coming to an end. Yet, though the Manchu era was a time of political and military decline, its cultural

achievements are unquestionable. In 1720 the Jesuit Father Regis completed the first scientifically-drawn map of China and in 1764 the official geography of the empire was published in a number of volumes. Other publications included a great encyclopedia of Chinese learning (1726) in 1,628 volumes, commentaries on numerous chronicles, historical works and annals, and also the great 36-volume Book of oracles.

The novel, the novella and, most of all, the play flourished. The Peking Opera displayed all the splendor and melodiousness of the East.

In painting the landscape painting of the "four Wangs" reached a peak of perfection in extreme restriction of artistic means and delicacy of brush strokes. Through European missionaries such as the Italian Giuseppe Castiglione the shapes and motifs of the European rococo style found their way into Chinese mural painting, and thus arose the Manchu court style.

The field of porcelain was at first dominated by the green glazes of Ts'ang-yao ceramics, then by the "ox-blood" porcelains of the Lang-yao school. Under the influence of the western style and richness of coloring the Manchu porcelain painting of the eighteenth and nineteenth centuries finally became polychromatic, with a wealth of motifs, colors and decorations.

But all these things, temples and palaces, porcelain, carpets, lacquer-work, bronzes, ivories and literature, could not conceal the fact that they were only the thin silk of a screen hiding rigid and outmoded formalism, corruption, decay and backwardness.

The stormy winds of time would tear down this flimsy screen of declining culture. Behind it a new China was struggling to be born.

Left: the Empress Tzu-Hsi, last great ruler of the Manchu dynasty.

Right: Dr. Sun Yat-sen, first leader of the Republic of China.

8 The Republic

The decline of the Manchu dynasty and the long series of humiliations at the hands of foreign powers, against a background of increasing social tensions and the rising hatred of the Ming Chinese for the Manchu regime, produced time and time again outbreaks of rebellion, conspiracies and new political factions. Moreover, with the gradual adoption of European ways, technology and education, with the founding of modern schools and universities, the dissemination of European ideas by mission schools, the building of modern hospitals, factories, railroads and a general adjustment to the world market and world trade routes, a young generation was growing up, fired with revolutionary ideas. Teachers, professors and students were those who shouted loudest for radical change. Many of them had studied in Japan, Europe and especially in the USA, where they came in contact with democratic and socialist ideas.

In 1905 a certain Dr. Sun Yat-sen, a doctor trained in Japan, the USA and England, gathered together the leaders of the revolutionary factions in Shanghai, actively aided by the Japanese nationalist party, Genyosha. Dr. Sun Yat-sen was the son of a Christian tenant farmer, worked as a doctor in Macao and Canton, and in 1894 founded an "Association for the Reunification and Restoration of China". He now transformed his association and other revolutionary groups into the T'ung-meng-hui or General League. His "Three People's Principles", which were later to have far-reaching repercussions which their author may not have anticipated, became the basis of the new party's program:

"1. Nationality: the overthrow of the Manchu dynasty and the foundation of a Chinese Republic.

2. The People's Authority: the ex-

ercise of the people's authority by a parliament.

3. The People's Livelihood: protection of the nation's livelihood by just distribution of land, restriction of capitalism and abolition of the overriding rights of foreign powers".

Time after time Dr. Sun Yat-sen's movement organised new outbreaks of rebellion, but they were conspiracies hatched in an inexpert, theoretical and dilettante manner by intellectuals and fuelled by ideology, discussion and wishful thinking. They were almost always betrayed in advance, and so poor was their preparation that they could be nipped in the bud.

Dr. Sun often directed the conspiracies from Japan, which was also the revolutionaries' best supplier of arms.

In March 1911 another attempted putsch was being prepared in Canton. Students and intellectuals held almost open debates on the subject, spied on by the Manchu secret police. On the evening of 29th March groups of badly-armed young people suddenly stormed the palace of the viceroy and were overwhelmed by a superior force of troops in the inner courtyard. 72 rebels, almost all of them students, were killed, the rest, a dozen or so, captured and later beheaded.

When these dreadful events became known in Japan, Dr. Sun Yat-sen wrote inflammatory articles for American and Japanese newspapers. One of his supporters, 24-year-old Lieutenant Chiang Kai-shek, who had just completed his training at the Tokyo Military Academy, left Japan to take an active part in the revolutionary struggle.

Chiang Kai-shek was born on 3rd October 1887 in Chekiang. He came of a good family and chose a military career. Even as a schoolboy and cadet

Chinese army maneuvers in 1907. China begins to modernise.

Top left: demonstration by
Chinese students (members of the
Kuomintang) in America.
Below: China's first National
Congress April 1912, in the center
President Yüan Shih-k'ai.
Right: Yüan Shih-k'ai, first President
of the Republic of China.

90

he had been a member of the "Tung-meng-hui".

He returned to China at exactly the right moment. The scandal of the Peking-Hangchow-Canton railroad was stirring people's emotions. The government had financed the construction of this railroad with funds raised by the Chinese people and had then transferred the operating concession to foreign companies. Chiang Kai-shek, the military leader of the revolutionary staff and Dr. Sun Yat-sen's representative, Ch'en Ch'i-mei, immediately laid plans for a new uprising. They chose the centrally situated city of Wu-Chang on the Yangtze as its focal point, as it contained much new industrial plant and large numbers of coolies. In the night of 11th October they launched their attack on the governor's palace, this time with efficient, military planning, captured it and gained the upper hand in Wu-Chang by means of bloody street-fighting. For the first time the revolutionaries

controlled a major city. The capture of Wu-Chang was a beacon-light. Dissidents in other parts of China rose in rebellion as well. The rebellion broke out in the province of Honan. In the city of Chang-sha the rebels set up barricades and fought the advancing Tartar troops of the government.

Amongst the students of Changsha's teacher training college the young Mao-Tse-Tung, from the village of Shao-shan in Honan, rose to prominence. His father, formerly a soldier in the army of the Manchu general Yuan Shih-k'ai, had returned to his home village and lived as a poor peasant. He wanted his son to be a teacher.

Mao, who even then knew several foreign languages and read European, Russian and American works on politics, Socialism and revolution, had a reputation as a rebel. Within a few days the rebellion of Wu-Chang and Chang-sha spread to the provinces of Hupei, Anhwei, Honan and

Dr. Sun Yat-sen's tomb near Nanking.

Chekiang. In the city of Hangchow, which he knew well, Chiang Kai-shek triumphed. Shortly before Christmas 1911 Nanking fell to the rebels.

Now Dr. Sun Yat-sen, who had heard the great news while in the USA, came hurrying back to China and arrived in Shanghai on Christmas Eve. A committee of the "Tung-meng-hui" begged him to serve his country as "Provisional President". Representatives of seventeen southern (Ming) provinces elected him to this office.

Confronted by this situation the Manchu court in Peking recalled the only man capable of arresting the avalanche of revolution – Marshal Yuan Shih-k'ai. He had formerly commanded the European-armed Chinese troops and had made himself popular by demanding reforms. The Manchu mandarins had exiled him.

Yuan Shih-k'ai returned to Peking and took over the leadership of the modernised military units. He thought that the situation was one of dynastic change and considered the time ripe to take over the Throne of Heaven himself. He acted with great cunning, forcing the Manchu government to resign on 12th February 1912 and proclaiming the setting up of a republic. So as not to endanger the cause of freedom in this hour of tension, Dr. Sun Yat-sen resigned his office, allowed himself to be fobbed off with a subordinate post in the new government and helped to establish the Marshal-President as political leader.

Dr. Sun Yat-sen now reorganised his Tung-meng-hui movement as a popular political party: the first western-type party in the Far East. The party was called "Kuomintang" and was a nationalist popular movement with three principles: nationalism, democracy and Socialism.

Dr. Sun Yat-sen's supporters were disappointed by the results of the revolution. Many accepted the offices and military commissions offered them by Yuan Shih-k'ai's government, but others left the country. Chiang Kai-shek returned to the Tokyo Military Academy.

When they parted, Dr. Sun Yat-sen gave Chen-Ch'i-mei this advice about Chiang: "Watch that young man carefully. I do not think that the revolution is at an end."

In the years that followed Marshal Yuan Shih-k'ai built up not only a strong military force in the North but also an increasingly absolute power as president. He completely dominated the two-chamber system of the pseudo-republic.

Against this republic the Kuomintang-led southern provinces, the Ming Chinese, rose in 1913 in a second and third wave of revolution. Troops put down these uprisings and President Yuan Shih-k'ai expelled the Kuomintang from parliament and in 1914 even abolished it.

When the First World War broke out, Japan, in violation of Chinese neutrality, landed troops to capture the German bases on the Shantung peninsula and the port of Kiaochow. Yuan Shih-k'ai, faced with a 21-point Japanese ultimatum, gave in and accepted it. The former German possessions in Shantung now fell into Japanese hands. China was even forced to declare war on the Central Powers, Germany and Austria, and provide battalions of coolies for the theaters of war in Mesopotamia, France and Africa. The Treaty of Versailles awarded the bases on the Shantung peninsula to Japan.

This new humiliation caused a wave of anti-Japanese feeling in China. President Yuan Shih-k'ai, who in 1916 was on the verge of realising his

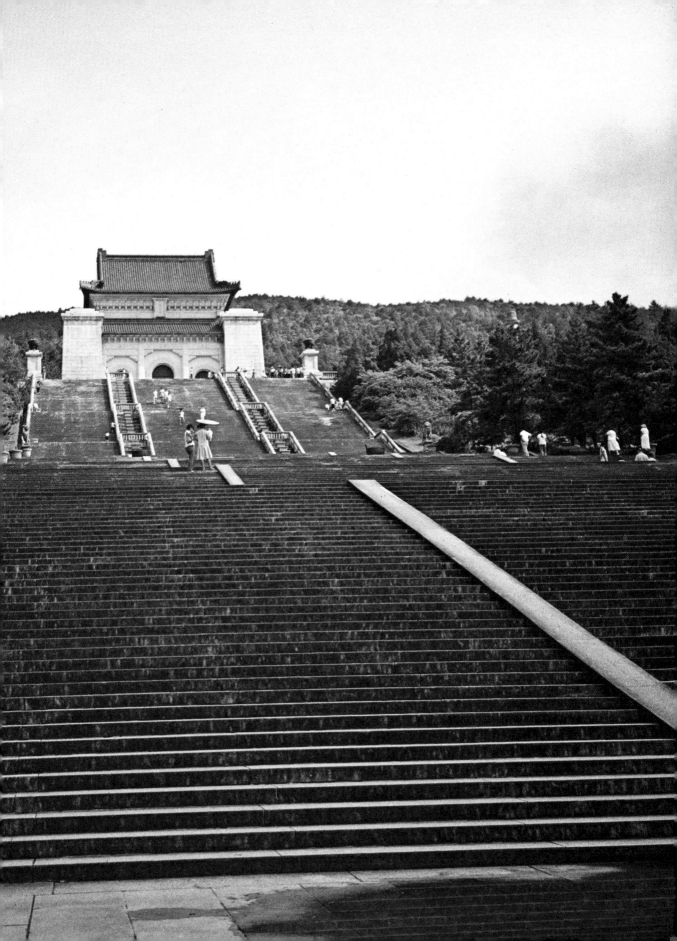

President Yüan Shih-k'ai with the diplomatic corps.

General Chiang Kai-shek with a delegation of Peking students who have presented him with a sword of honor.

own designs on the imperial throne, was unequal to the Japanese blow to his prestige. All the southern provinces rose against him, the very provinces who supported Dr. Sun Yat-sen. On 6th June 1916 Marshal Yuan Shih-k'ai was murdered by a Chinese nationalist.

In 1920, after the First World War, Dr. Sun Yat-sen was elected president of a South China Republic independent of Peking and the Manchu provinces, with its capital at Canton. The civil war between North and South dragged on. Throughout the country warlords now appeared, ambitious generals and bandit chiefs, who fought each other. In the North General Chang Tso-lin set up a dictatorship.

These events led to a general radicalisation of parties and political leaders. In Russia in 1917 the Socialist revolution triumphed. Lenin, Trotsky, Kirov and Stalin appeared and made their appeals to the world. The Soviet Union fought back against the Western Allies and Japan in the War of Intervention—a shining example for China. Dr. Sun Yat-sen, after appointing the newly returned Chiang Kai-shek commandant of the modern military academy at Whampoa near Canton, then sent him, his right-hand man, to Moscow and sought a fraternal alliance with the Soviet Union. The Kuomintang party moved to the left and collaborated with the Communists.

In the meantime Mao Tse-tung had become an assistant librarian in Peking, obtained in only a few years promotion to mandarin of the highest rank and devoted himself to the study of communist doctrines. He adopted

many of the ideas of Marxism-Leninism but combined them in the Chinese fashion with the lessons learned from China's history over the previous two and a half thousand years. The experiences of the Lords of Chou, of the philosopher Wang Yang and Meng-K'o, the procedures and systems used by Chancellor Li during the Tsin period (when there were People's Communes, cells and collective work) became relevant once again.

Imitating the counsel of the ancient philosopher Wang Shang (Tsin dynasty, 240 B.C.) he advised his followers to join the Kuomintang and to transform it from within. In the meantime he had moved to the gigantic coastal city of Shanghai and there, on 1st July 1921, he founded the Chinese Communist Party, whose First Secre-

tary he became. Moscow sent the secret agent Maring (real name Sneevliet) to advise Mao in the power-struggle to come.

In 1923 the Kuomintang, led by Dr. Sun Yat-sen and Chiang Kai-shek, made plain its support for the Third International and Soviet Communism. Chiang Kai-shek went back to Moscow to study the now firmly-established Soviet system.

In 1924 China's first National Congress met in Canton. The Kuomintang had scored an overwhelming victory in the election of its members, and it chose Dr. Sun Yat-sen as president. German and Russian instructors came to South China to reorganise air transport, the army and navy. The Soviet Union was also the first Great Power to renounce all war reparations

due from the "Opium" and "Lorcha" Wars, from the days of the Boxer Rebellion and the unfair treaties forced on China in the heyday of imperialism. A close alliance seemed to be growing up between the Soviet Union and the Kuomintang, two great families of peoples who controlled their own destinies.

The demands increased. Mao Tsetung's Communists aimed at large-scale land reform, equalisation of financial burdens by expropriation of capitalists and the creation of an armed peasant militia. People's democracy was on the march.

Dr. Sun Yat-sen died suddenly on 1st March 1925. From then on the Kuomintang was led by Chiang Kai-shek (now back from Moscow), Wang Ching-wei and the Russian Borodin.

Mao was now able to set about translating his ideas into reality. With the aid of his peasant militia he founded the first Chinese Soviet Republic and the first "People's Communes" in the provinces of Kiangsi and Fukien, which he largely controlled. The Kuomintang was increasingly split between its left and moderate right wings.

Chiang Kai-shek, wielding great influence as generalissimo of the Kuomintang armies, changed his attitudes, too. He had returned from Moscow a convinced friend of the Soviet system, but he now viewed with concern the growing influence of Soviet agents such as Borodin, Maring, Joffé and others. In Canton, where he had his headquarters, he made the acquaintance of the daughter of Sung, a

97

Chinese representation of Japanese atrocities during the Mukden Incident in Manchuria, 1932.

Shensi, the destination of the Mao's "Long March" (1935–36).

multi-millionaire capitalist. Her sister had married Dr. Sun Yat-sen. His attitude to Socialism underwent a change when he married Mei-ling on 1st December 1927. He made a radical change of front and turned against Mao's Communists. A Sung became Minister of Finance.

Thus it came about that the Red Army led by Mao and his colleague Chou En-lai and Chiang's Kuomintang army suddenly became enemies. The old Kuomintang collapsed.

China was in turmoil—provincial generals, revolutionaries, Kuomintang Rightists, bandits, gang leaders surged through the provinces, plun-dering and burning. The proclamation of a provisional constitution on 5th May 1931 in Nanking had only a theoretical effect. Chiang Kai-shek's armies dominated the South but were powerless against the Communist provinces and in the North. The Japanese, who had in the meantime become apt pupils of European and American imperialism, exploited China's weakness. After an armed clash in Mukden, Japanese troops began to occupy Manchuria. In 1932 their vastly-superior navy even landed at Shanghai after a heavy bombardment. On 18th February the Japanese declared Manchuria an independent territory under their "protection". The last descendant of the Manchu dynasty, the 28-year-old Emperor Pu-i, was made ruler of "Manchukuo".

Was it time for a colonial partition of China? Chiang Kai-shek understood very well that China could only defend itself if it were united. So he made every effort to complete the "Unification Campaign" against Mao's Communists, which had been in progress since 1927. In October 1934 he began an attack on the Communist provinces of Fukien and Kiangsi.

Here Mao, Chu The, Chou En-lai and Peng Huai had set up a kind of popular democracy. The "Red Army"

99

Generalissimo Chiang Kai-shek inspecting the political cadres of his army in Chungking.

Japanese parade in conquered Hankow.

had a force of 100,000 well-disciplined soldiers. Mao was elected Chairman of the party and Russian influence was as yet slight.

But Chiang Kai-shek, unlike Mao, had modern tanks, artillery and planes. When he opened an attack from all sides, the Communists were heavily defeated. In the end all that remained for the hard core of Mao's supporters was flight en masse, taking their families with them.

The "Long March" began. First almost a million people set off with carts, ponies and pushcarts to escape encirclement by Kuomintang troops. The journey of nearly 8,000 miles, a third of the earth's circumference, took them through plains, over flooding rivers with demolished bridges, through swamps, impassable mountains with passes 12,000 feet high, through storms, rain, ice and snow. In crossing rivers they lost food supplies, ammu-

nition and heavy arms. They were constantly under artillery fire, were defenseless against attacks from the air and had often to turn and fight.

In those days of heroism and naked survival Mao wrote his poem on the "Long March". Nowadays every Chinese child can recite it:

"The Red Army had no fear
of the hardships of the long march,
nor of rivers or mountains,
though they raised a thousand
    obstacles.
The five mountain ranges
curved and twisted.
High stood Wu-meng, Raven's
    Grave,
through whose mud we trudged
    forwards.
Through overhanging cliffs
the Yangtze flows in hot haste.
The cold iron chain-bridge spanned
    the Tatu.

Top left: American instructors helping with the modernisation of the Chinese army.
Bottom: American transport planes bringing supplies for the Chungking government.
Below: Japanese soldiers storming a burning Chinese town.

We were even happier to see from afar
the snows of Min-shan.
And when the Army marched through,
it seemed to look at us with joy."

Mao reached Yennan in the northern province of Shensi with only one-fifth of his force—200,000 men. For years the clay caves of Yennan were Mao's headquarters, here his army set up a new popular democracy and turned itself into a formidable force.

Chiang Kai-shek's campaign to destroy the Communists was stopped by the "Sian Incident". When Chiang visited the commander of his Northern Army on 12th December 1936, the latter took him prisoner and forced him, instead of continuing his campaign against Mao, to negotiate with the Communists, represented by Chou En Lai. From now on the national struggle against the Japanese was to be a joint operation.

The war against the Japanese lasted from 1937 to 1945, having merged smoothly into the Second World War. Both came to an end at the same time.

The course of events brought about in 1937 a non-aggression pact between China and Russia. When the USA entered the war the Chinese became part of the Allied camp. Vast quantities of American aid enabled Chiang Kai-shek to continue the struggle against Japan. To transport these Lend-Lease goods in safety, the Americans and British built the fantastic Burma Road over six peaks of the Himalaya range to Chungking, Chiang's new capital.

Because of the ever-increasing corruption in Kuomintang circles, about a third of all these weapons, supplies and equipment came into the hands of the "Balu Army", who from their base in Yenan fought the Japanese as allies of Chiang and the Americans. The

103

"Balu Army" was in fact Mao and his Communists.

The advance of the Japanese forces captured almost all the important places near China's coast—Nanking, Shanghai, Hankow and Hangchow. China fought back with guerilla warfare and sabotage, and the Japanese attack petered out in China's immense spaces.

Nevertheless in 1938 they succeeded in setting up a "Reformed Govern- ment of the Republic of China" in Nanking, headed by the turncoat Wang Ching-wei.

Immense suffering afflicted the "Middle Kingdom". Japanese squa- drons bombed its cities, fighters drove masses of people along its roads, Japanese and Chinese troops com- mitted unspeakable atrocities. The Second World War shook the whole of the Far East. Everywhere the imperial and colonial system collapsed, either under Japanese invasion or in the course of the war.

Japan was fighting for its very life. The USA advanced through the is- lands of the Pacific, and the war en- tered its final phase.

Chiang Kai-shek and Kuomintang China glimpsed for the first time in twenty years the silver lining of peace to come. And in the North their allies, Mao Tse-tung and his Balu Army, tasted victory.

9 Red China

As the collapse of Japan and the consequent victory and peace for China approached, Chiang Kai-shek, his Chungking government and the Kuomintang party had already largely thrown away whatever chances they might have had of bringing about a new order in China.

According to the ideas of the earlier Kuomintang under Dr. Sun Yat-sen and young Chiang Kai-shek, the chaos of the Manchu dynasty was to be replaced by the harmony of a social democracy and usher in a new era in Chinese history. In the beginning all the leading revolutionaries had been Socialists.

But ever since Chiang Kai-shek had married into the richest capitalist family in China, the Sungs, by taking Mei-ling as his wife, he had turned away more and more from Socialism. Even in his Kuomintang government of 1931 there were six members of the Sung family, including Mei-ling's brother as Minister of Finance.

Bankers, large landowners, industrialists and businessmen took the place of the Manchu mandarins. Money-lenders were allowed to exploit the poverty of peasants mercilessly, tough land agents were permitted to squeeze out excessive farm rents, with the complicity of the government businessmen made money out of the trade in coolies and in girls for the "flower boats".

Corruption ruled supreme. Appointments to official posts were made on grounds of family relationships, connections and bribery. When in the war against Japan the USA pumped vast quantities of weapons and supplies into China, the racketeers flourished to an incredible extent.

Left: Generalissimo Chiang Kai-shek with General Joseph Stilwell,
Commander of the American forces in China, Burma and India.
Right: the Japanese forces in China capitulate on 9th September 1945
in Nanking.

Chungking generals sold American supplies not only to the Communists in Yennan and to the warlords but even to the Japanese!

Chiang Kai-shek seemed helpless to prevent the decay of the Kuomintang and the corruption of its officials. He had ceased to be a Socialist. In any case the hopes of the people, exploited and living in the utmost poverty, were now focussed in a different direction. According to American figures, three million Chinese died of famine each winter in the last ten years of Kuomintang rule.

While Chiang Kai-shek's regime was weakening, Mao Tse-tung and his Communist movement became more and more respected.

When General Stillwell, Special Envoy and leader of the American Military Mission, warned Washington in 1944 of the Communist peril in China and denounced Kuomintang corruption, he was ruthlessly dismissed by Roosevelt.

In February 1945 Churchill, Roosevelt and Stalin met at Yalta to decide on a world political settlement in anticipation of the war's approaching end. Amongst other things the "Big Three" decided that each enemy army was to surrender to the Allied force against which it had been fighting. When on the following day this passage was provisionally signed and translated into English, Stalin had it altered so that it ran as follows, with specific reference to China: "The Japanese armies on the mainland are to capitulate to the local Chinese military commander". The Americans found the text acceptable, realising that at the time of the capitulation Marshal Chiang Kai-shek could not be everywhere at once.

By agreeing to this the USA practically underwrote the foundation of Red China! For when in August 1945, after the use of the atomic bomb and the Russian advance, the Japanese laid down their arms, it was naturally Mao Tse-tung's Balu Army which received the capitulation of the Japanese Kwantung Army in the North.

The Kwantung Army was the only army in the Far East still completely intact and fit for combat, complete with all its weapons, supply bases and Manchurian war industries. Mao inherited it. But to turn the hundreds of thousands of Communist troops of the Balu Army plus the modern arms and equipment of the Kwantung Army into a really efficient weapon for fighting a civil war, even Mao needed three or four years for reorganisation and training. The Americans provided this for him.

Propaganda poster showing men of the Chinese Red Army attacking.

In the Fall of 1945 Chiang Kai-shek and his numerically far superior Kuomintang forces immediately resumed the fight against the Communists in the North, instead of devoting their energies to the reconstruction of the country. General Marshall arrived and began negotiations to stop further hostilities between these two "allies" of the USA. When Chiang in February 1947 nevertheless set his armies in motion and occupied Mao's headquarters in Yenan, the Americans departed in great disappointment and in retaliation suspended all aid.

On the 19th April 1948 Chiang Kai-shek was again elected first President of the Chinese Republic by the National Assembly in Nanking. The northern provinces, which had meanwhile been taken over by Communist partisans and the rapidly re-equipping Balu Army, did not join in, however. On 28th December 1946 Mao formally suspended the Kuomintang constitution in his provinces. On 10th October 1947 he proclaimed the basic program of Chinese agrarian reform: total expropriation of large landowners, seizure of the land by the pea-

sants who tilled it, abolition of mortgages and extortionate rates of interest—a program which was given an enthusiastic welcome by poor villagers, propertyless coolies and exploited peasant farmers.

On 25th December 1947 Mao's mass army went over from the defensive to the offensive.

At the time when, in the atmosphere of worsening East-West conflict, NATO was being founded in Europe, Mao's flood of Communist soldiery was already over the Yangtze-Kiang. It was now too late for effective inter-

Idealised representation of China's progress under Mao Tse-tung.

vention by the USA and Europe on behalf of Chiang, now suddenly more important in the field of world politics. Almost unhindered the Red Army completed its victorious advance to the South. Exhausted by thirty years of war and civil war, the people welcomed Mao's troops as liberators. Chiang's armies broke up.

On 23rd April 1949 Nanking, the southern capital, was stormed, an epic event later to be portrayed in the ballet "The East is Red". On 27th May Mao's troops had already reached the outskirts of Shanghai. It was to this great port that Generalissimo Chiang Kai-shek had retreated with his elite divisions. Huge crowds of refugees, mainly upper middle class people, intellectuals, financiers, landowners and Kuomintang officials, crowded onto the quays of Shanghai.

Because of the shortage of petrol, Mao's armies mainly used horses, mules and carts for transportation, or went on foot. Nevertheless whole Nationalist divisions and army corps laid down their arms before them, and towns threw open their gates to them without firing a shot.

In his study of Mao Tse-tung Lük-kenhaus writes: "The number of defectors from the ranks of the Kuomintang increased by leaps and bounds. High officials and army officers freely offered their services to the advancing Red Army. It was the debacle of a decaying system in which for many personal advantage was more important than duty". It was a case of "sauve qui peut".

Whilst the artillery thundered around Shanghai Chiang embarked his supporters and units of the National army for those areas of Chinese territory protected by the sea, principally for Formosa. After an adventurous life as revolutionary, hero

of the liberation, soldier, statesman, head of government and head of state, Chiang left the mainland, never to enter his native land again.

On 21st September 1949, following the decision of the National Congress, Mao proclaimed the Chinese People's Republic. Article 1 of its "Organic Law" reads:

"The Chinese People's Republic is a state with a democratic people's dictatorship, led by the working classes, founded on unification of workers and peasants. It unites all democratic classes and different nationalities within the country".

The new constitution distinguished four classes—workers, peasants, petty bourgeoisie and capitalists. The proletariat ruled the state and possessed full rights of citizenship, whilst the rest, second-class citizens who were necessary and useful for the time being, had only duties. Supreme power was wielded by a party Central Committee limited to 56 members, which had legislative and executive functions. Thirty ministries in Peking were subordinate to it. Mao Tse-tung became President and Chou En-lai Prime Minister.

The fighting lasted until the end of 1949 in the coastal areas, then the last refugees and army units left for Formosa. The Red Armies occupied a number of off-shore islands including Hainan. But their path to Formosa was barred: now the Americans sent in their Seventh Fleet and put a barrier of steel and guns between the opposing factions.

Whilst the victorious Communist troops were pouring through the mountain valleys of Szechwan and Yunnan, making a Long March in reverse, Mao declared that he would also occupy Tibet, considering it a former Chinese province, just as he intended to regain all former Chinese provinces

The troops of Red China enter Tibet and re-unite this province, held by the
Chinese for centuries, with the renascent "Middle Kingdom".

and border territories from the Imperialists and Colonialists.

India, only recently given its independence by the British and engaged in reconstruction and reorganisation, was in December 1949 the first state to grant China diplomatic recognition, a step which would take the USA a further twenty years. Pendit Nehru expressed the opinion that China was historically entitled to a certain degree of sovereignty over Tibet.

At the beginning of 1950 Great Britain recognised Red China. A number of European and non-European countries followed this example. Encouraged by these diplomatic gains, the USSR proposed that the United Nations strip Chiang's Nationalists on Formosa of the right to represent China's interests at future meetings of that organisation even on the Security Council.

This move was defeated by the American veto, and Nationalist China remained a member of the UN. Now, thrown out of the Middle Kingdom,

Chiang became an ally of the USA which recognised him alone as the representative of China. Mao's China, in such great isolation, replied with a violent propaganda campaign against the "US paper tiger".

A further twenty years had to pass before the USA was prepared to come to terms with the realities of the political situation and accept the existence of a rapidly-developing Red China rising to Great Power and World Power status, and to take up diplomatic relations with this, the largest state on earth. Then they would be forced by the facts of world politics to give up their old ally Chiang Kai-shek, maneuver him out of the UN and withdraw their protection from him.

But until that moment came the Chiang Kai-shek Formosa-based state was able to develop into a considerable economic and industrial power, build up a large modern army and even after Chiang's death (1975) for a while maintain its position relative to the real China.

In February 1950 Mao went to Moscow and concluded a treaty of friendship and assistance with Stalin. The USSR, though its resources were fully engaged in its reconstruction program, was the only industrial power in the world willing to help devastated China. 60 million roubles flowed into China and 5,000 Russian specialist advisers entered the country to implement its industrialisation program.

The Communist take-over in China did not come about without bloodshed and cruelty. When the Red Army marched in it was usually joined by the poor of the countryside, the coolies from the towns and the partisans who had long since infiltrated into the area. They took their revenge on the erstwhile exploiters, on corrupt Kuomintang officials, on everybody suspected of having been capitalists, moneylenders, bankers, debt-collectors or hirelings of foreign countries. Mao, who in his writings had often spoken of preparing the way for the people's revenge, later gave the number of victims as 750,000. That is a considerable number, but it looks very modest compared with the American estimate of 16 millions dead as the outcome of the work of the revolutionary tribunals.

In cities like Shanghai or Canton the executions were announced on the radio every day. Everybody could hear the rage of the mob, the pistol shots and the death-cries of the victims over the public loud-speaker system.

In the course of liberation from "Imperialism and Colonialism" many missionaries, European doctors and technical experts aiding the Chinese people were also killed. However, these events should not be interpreted in the Cold War manner as political atrocities. The often severe measures

of a tightly-organised "liberation dictatorship" were offset by constant striving to achieve a consensus within China. All sections of the population were encouraged to co-operate. In consolidating his power, i.e. that of the Chinese Communist Party, Mao tried to avoid unnecessary suffering. This was a pragmatic policy clearly distinct from that of Soviet communism.

In 1950, immediately after the victory of the revolution, Mao began to put into practice the agrarian reform he had promised. A hundred million poor peasants received a piece of land of their own. Previously the rich landowners and city capitalists had forced small farmers to hand over 60—70% of the produce as the rent of a small piece of land. The landowners, consisting of only 16% of the rural population, had owned over 60% of China's land.

Mao began by basing his power on the small peasants who revered him. But soon the next step followed. The peasants were organised in rural co-operatives, which took over the private ownership of land. The fields were cultivated jointly, as in the days of the Chou and the Tsin. Setting up tractor stations made large-scale agriculture possible. In 1955, when Mao was firmly in the saddle, he took the bold step of setting up "people's communes" everywhere. By 1968 private ownership of land had been totally abolished.

Everywhere the slogans waved: "Jen-min kuang-sheh-hao!"—"The People's Commune is a fine thing!"

For that too, was a concomitant of Mao's Communism—the re-education of the whole population by unceasing propaganda. On the wallposters, in leaflets, in the widely-distributed "Little Red Book" ("Thoughts of Chairman Mao"), in

the outpourings of the public loudspeakers, in the cinemas, the re-education classes, the schools and universities there was only one voice, that of Mao and the Communists.

"They each combine the agriculture, trade, industry, education and militia organisation of a district. The People's Communes are organised as cells (just as in Li Ssu's day) fused into the Communist block. The Chinese regard that as the first stage of pure Communism . . ."

Work was organised on military lines, so that school children turned themselves into highly-disciplined military cadres. The Chinese went off to work in squads, companies and brigades, without regard to age or sex. With a hundred thousand hands they achieved what in the USA or Europe is normally done by huge machines: they constructed vast dams, flood protection embankments, new rice terraces, they built highways and railroads through mountain ranges, spanned the vast Yangtze with a technical masterpiece of a bridge, built up industrial combines and created new factories, just as their ancestors had built the Great Wall.

When the peasant went to work he took not only his spade but his rifle, the machine-gun as well as the plow was taken to the fields. In the breaks between work the squad practised drill, in the factory yards military commands rang out and even in the kindergartens there was pre-military training. A traveller of the sixties, Gillhausen-Held, describes this China devoted to almost fanatical reconstruction: "they swarm, cluster, split up again into strings, into little columns, finding their way around obstacles, coming to a halt a ditches and then hastily resuming their work . . . They mill about in an area about 500

115

Demonstration by Red Guards with Mao's "Little Red Book".

Young Red Guards demonstrate with Mao's "Little Red Book" and banners.

yards square, fetching white sand from all sides for the dam. Each one carries on his shoulder a bamboo pole with baskets slung from the ends. On each journey they transport a hundredweight of sand . . .!"

The age of the "blue ants" had come, for this new nation was dressed almost uniformly in suits of blue linen. It was difficult from a distance to tell girls from boys, women from men—pigtails had long since disappeared, but now they all wore their hair medium-length.

At first Mao aimed to bring about not only agrarian reform and an adequate supply of food for the population, but also a rapid build-up of heavy industry, helped by Russian specialists and machinery and by credits from the Eastern Block. But for the USSR of the fifties and sixties iron and steel were scarce commodities. Moreover the Soviet Union had in the meantime realised that by supporting Red China it was not only fostering a rival for the role of leader of World Communism but also strengthening a potential adversary. For in the speeches and newspaper articles of the Chinese leaders one could already detect tones of displeasure at the "unequal treaties" of Imperialist and Colonialist days, in which Czarist Russia was the chief culprit. Whilst all the great Colonialist countries of the past, Great Britain, France, Spain and the USA, had long since granted independence to their dependencies and colonies, the Soviet Union was the only one to keep a firm grip on all the territory it had conquered and occupied from the Caucasus to Turkestan, Siberia and Manchuria. The Chinese had not forgotten that parts of Mon-

Mao with Defense Minister Lin Piao, who ranked second after Mao. Several years later Lin died mysteriously on a flight to Russia.

golia, Tannu-Tuva, the Amur province, the Ussuri province, Kamchatka and other border areas had once been under Chinese sovereignly.

Relations with the USSR became more and more troubled, especially as Moscow tried to increase its influence on events in China. One day the Chinese suddenly sent all Russian advisers, agents and party comrades packing. The Russians stopped all economic aid immediately.

China's policies were already at variance with those of the Soviet Union in South-East Asia—in North and South Vietnam, Laos, Cambodia, Burma and Thailand. The People's Republic of China became the model and support of many Third World countries which were suffering from the consequences of colonialism and an unfairly-organised world economy.

Hostility towards the USA decreased more and more, until it finally ceased, after the preparatory phase of "ping-pong diplomacy", on the establishment of informal diplomatic relations between the two states. The new main adversary was the USSR.

Once again Mao tried a "Great Leap Forward". Attempts were made to fill the enormous gap in iron and steel production by setting up village smelting plants and the collection of scrap metal. In the amazing efforts made by industry to catch up with the other World Powers by means of round-the-clock work in the heavy industry sector, the plant was overloaded and hundreds of works saw their equipment break down. No spares or replacements were now available from the USSR, and Japan, the USA, and Europe only cautiously

March-past of the Red Militia in the People's Stadium in Peking.

光荣的、伟大
修正主义!打倒各国反动派!
自 聞

resumed the supply of industrial goods.

Despite this, China managed to set up huge power stations in Szechwan and to the amazement of the world produced its own atomic bomb. But Mao had long since throttled back on heavy industrial production. He had time to turn China into the kind of World Power in keeping with her population of 800 millions. What Russia achieved from 1917 to 1960, a mere 43 years, with a population then composed of 95% unskilled peasants, China would also bring about with its people steeped for centuries in artistic, technical and fine craft skills.

Again and again Mao appealed to the Chinese to support the party line, aggressive Communism and ideological purity. True, when soon after Stalin's death and the break with Russia the "Great Leap Forward" failed, he did proclaim that from henceforward agriculture, followed by craft and light industry, was to have a higher priority than heavy industry, armaments and large-scale projects. He was also successful in doing away with those things which had most sorely afflicted the Chinese people in the past—hunger, homelessness and cold. Nowadays, nobody in China starved and everyone who worked had somewhere to live and security. But the very fact that the problem of poverty had been solved had the effect of making party officials and the well-fed began to deviate from the line of "pure Socialism" and become fat and lazy.

In 1952 Mao carried out his "Campaign of the Five Evils". It was directed against those guilty of economic sabotage, tax evasion, corruption, exploitation and espionage. The number of suicides caused is unknown, and there are no exact figures for the masses of convictions.

121

A year later the intellectuals went through their own screening process, and about 190,000 counter-revolutionaries, mostly writers, professors, former Confucians, Christians and leading employees were liquidated. From this time onwards red flags flew from every temple and church.

In February 1957 Mao surprised the world by a speech advocating a kind of free democracy and announcing the slogan: "Let a hundred flowers bloom!"

For a short time it was even possible to make mild criticisms of the party itself, and differing opinions on politics, art and literature were expressed. But then the gates slammed shut. All that was left for the incautious critics was suicide, self-criticism or condemnation by the courts. The ever-repeated waves of the "Cultural Revolution" ensured that the party's blood was kept briskly circulating, that abuses and opposition were swept away and the young, filled with revolutionary spirit, returned to Mao's "pure doctrine". This "Cultural Revolution" was directed most of all against those officials, intellectuals and officers who had grown lethargic and corrupt in their official positions.

Ever since the USA, under President Nixon, made the historic change in its policy and effected a reconciliation with Mao sealed in 1971 by Nixon's personal visit, its NATO allies and the European Common Market countries have ventured a friendly rapprochement with China. In 1971 the Chinese People's Republic was admitted to the U.N. and was given the Security Council seat formerly occupied by Nationalist China, now based on Formosa. Today, more than three decades after the Chinese Revolution, nobody can possibly overlook the reborn and revitalised "Middle Kingdom". Composed of almost 800 million well-organised citizens, well on the way to becoming an industrial power of the first order, engaged in an expanding program of rocket and atomic projects, its interior strength more and more firmly consolidated, living in well-founded social equality, Red China can now repeat the achievements prefigured in the Han and T'ang periods. Chinese trade, Chinese military aid and Chinese policies are already having a radical effect on conditions in Vietnam, Laos, Thailand, Indonesia and Burma. China's shadow has not only fallen over the Siberian border provinces, Manchuria and North Korea but also over India, Pakistan and Iran. Its influence can be seen in the whole of Black Africa, in recent policies of the Common Market countries and most of all in Latin America.

It has become the third World Power alongside America and Russia. Even after the death of the two great dominant figures of the People's Republic (Chou and Mao both died in 1976), the political leadership of the country continued the same internal and external policies.

The liberalisation of China's foreign policy: President Nixon welcomed by Prime Minister Chou En-lai at Peking Airport.

Chronology

c. 2300 B.C.	Yang Shao period. Migration from the mainland to Japan.
2220–1650 B.C.	Hsia dynasty (legendary).
1650–1122 B.C.	Shang or Yin dynasty.
1122–255 B.C.	Chou dynasty.
1122–771 B.C.	Capital at Feng.
771–255 B.C.	Capital at Lo-yang.
551–479 B.C.	Kung Fu-Tzu.
c. 500 B.C.	Lao-Tzu.
330 B.C.	Shang Yang, political philosopher.
221–206 B.C.	Tsin dynasty.
218 B.C.	Great Wall begun.
up to 210 B.C.	Chinese armies advance into Vietnam, Yunnan and Mongolia.
206 B.C.–220 A.D.	Han dynasty.
127 B.C.	Hun campaigns. First rockets.
25–220 A.D.	Capital once again at Lo-yang.
73–102 A.D.	General Pan Chao in West Turkestan.
c. 100 A.D.	Invention of paper. Trade with Antiochia and Java.
220–265	Capital of the Southern Empire at Nanking.
265–420	Tsin dynasty. Capitals at Ch'ang-an and Lo-yang.
420–589	Invasions by Huns, Turks and Tungus.
581–618	Sui dynasty.
605–618	Emperor Yang the Cruel. Construction of Imperial Canal.
618–906	T'ang dynasty. Introduction of examination system and civil service.
600–621	Buddhism adopted throughout China.
670	Defeat at hands of Tibetans.
701–762	Poet Li Po.
755	Intrigues of the Lady Jade Ring (Yuang Kuei Fei). Uprisings.
845	Edict against Buddhist monks.
907–1123	The North dominated by Khitan.
960–1279	Sung dynasty.
966	Last great pilgrimage to India.
976–996	Emperor Tai Tsu. Unification of China.
1004–1064	China buys off its enemies. Foundation of academies.
1101–1125	Emperor Hui Tsung, the "Painter Emperor".
1124	Destruction of the Khitan. Ch'in attack Kaifeng.
1130	Ch'in state extends as far as the Yangtse.
1127–1162	Emperor Kao Tsung. Introduction of paper currency. Use of explosive weapons.
1211	Mongol attacks.
1213	Northern China overrun by Mongols.
1271–1294	Kublai Khan Emperor of China. Yüan dynasty.
1274–1292	Marco Polo visits China.
1311–1320	Emperor Jen Tsung.
1311–1374	Ni-Tsan, painter-philosopher. Drama flourishes.
1355–1368	Revolt of the "Red Kerchiefs".
1368	Capture of Peking.
1368–1644	Ming dynasty.
1375	Currency reform, paper money, construction of the Imperial Palace in Peking.
1378	Legal Code Ta-Ming-Ju
1403–1424	Extension of Great Wall begun. Construction of pagodas. Use of colored glazes on porcelain. Lacquer work. Culture flourishes.
1403–1434	Construction of fleet for use against Japan. Capital moved to Peking.
1550–1552	Japanese besiege Nanking and Canton.
1552	Death of St. Francis Xavier.
1557	Macao taken by Portuguese.
1580–1610	Father Matteo Ricci working in China.
1598–1677	Wang produces his famous paintings, Golden Age of drama.
1622	"White Lotus" secret society.
1644	Manchus take Peking. End of Ming dynasty.
1644–1912	Manchu dynasty.
1643	Father Schall director of Peking Observatory.
1662–1722	Emperor Sheng-Tsu.
1689	Treaty of Nerchinsk.

1720	Hong merchants established in Canton.
1736–1795	Emperor Kao-Tsung.
1740	Administrative reform.
1757	All Chinese ports closed to foreigners.
1774	Revival of the "White Lotus".
1791–1792	Campaign in Nepal.
1796–1820	Emperor Jen-Tsung.
1821–1830	Emperor Hsüan-Tsung.
1834	Abolition of East India Company's monopoly of trade with China.
1839	Imperial Commissioner Liu-Tse-Hsü confiscates opium.
1840–1842	Opium War. Hong Kong seized by British.
1850–1864	Taiping rebellion.
1857–1860	"Lorcha War". Canton in flames. Destruction of the Summer Palace in Peking.
1860	Peking Convention.
1862–1864	Taiping rebellion put down with the aid of European troops.
1870	Sun Yat-sen born.
1875–1908	Dowager Empress Tzu-Hsi.
1887	Chiang Kai-shek born.
1893	Mao Tse-tung born.
1894	First attempts at industrialisation.
1894–1895	Chino-Japanese War in Korea.
1898	Agitation for reform. "Boxer" secret society.
1900–1901	Boxer Rebellion. Europeans intervene in Peking.
1905	Sun Yat-sen in Japan.
1906	Chiang attempts uprising, then leaves for Japan.
1911	Revolution in China.
1912	Fall of the Manchu dynasty. China becomes a republic.
1917	China declares war on Germany. Civil war between North and South China. Conflicts between generals.
1919	Mao Tse-tung founds Chinese Communist Party.
1923	Dr. Sun Yat-sen seeks alliance with USSR and Communists.
1923–1926	Russian "Advisers" in China.
1925	Death of Dr. Sun Yat-sen. Mao and Chou En-lai set up first Soviet Republics in China.
1926	Chiang Kai-shek becomes generalissimo of the Canton Army.
1928	Chiang's northern campaign.
1931	Japanese occupation of Manchuria.
1932	Military coup d'état at Sian.
1934	"Manchukuo Empire" founded. Chiang's campaign against Mao (the "Long March"), lasting until 1935.
1936	Chiang arrested at Sian.
1937	Outbreak of Chino-Japanese war, which lasted until 1945.
1939	Completion of Burma Road.
1945	End of Second World War.
1948	Chiang becomes President. Mao victorious in North China.
1949	Mao conquers the whole of China. Chiang leaves for Formosa. China breaks with USA and UN.
1950–1953	Korean War. China intervenes.
1950–1960	Modernisation and industrialisation of China. Border dispute between India and China. Bombardment of Quemoy and Matsu.
1961	China produces atomic bomb. Introduction of People's Communes.
1962	New border disputes with India. China breaks with USSR.
1966	Cultural Revolution.
1968–1969	Border disputes with USSR.
1970	China's first satellite.
1972	Reconciliation with USA. China becomes member of UN.
1976	Death of Mao. Struggle against "Gang of Four".
1977	Hua becomes Mao's successor.